R.S.V.P.

Menus for Entertaining from People Who Really Know How

BY NAN KEMPNER

PHOTOGRAPHS BY QUENTIN BACON

CLARKSON POTTER/PUBLISHERS
NEW YORK

Published by Clarkson Potter/Publishers, New York, New York
Member of the Crown Publishing Group
Random House, Inc.
New York, Toronto, London, Sydney, Auckland
www.randomhouse.com

CLARKSON N. POTTER is a trademark and
POTTER and colophon are registered trademarks of
Random House, Inc.

Printed in China

Library of Congress Cataloging-in-Publication Data
    R.S.V.P.: menus for entertaining from people who really know
how / by Nan Kempner.—1st ed.
    1. Entertaining.   2. Cookery.   3. Menus.   I Title.
TX731.K4325 2000
642'4—dc21   99-055319

ISBN 0-609-60430-9

10 9 8 7 6 5 4 3 2 1

FIRST EDITION

Acknowledgments

The creation of this book was an exciting, interesting experience and a dream come true. As it is with any project, dreams come true with the help of many. To the following, my gratitude.

Ed Victor, the godfather of *R.S.V.P.* and a super agent. Thank you for your time, energy, and imagination on behalf of Sloan-Kettering and me.

Pam Krauss, my unflaggingly supportive editor and benevolent dictator.

Annette Tapert, who raced in on her white charger when I finally admitted to myself that a couple of college writing courses were just not enough.

Quentin Bacon, a photographer of outstanding talent who knew intuitively how to translate my thoughts into a visual presentation.

Darienne Sutton, food editor extraordinaire. Her enthusiasm for life and capacity for enjoyment is unsurpassable.

For the entire team at Clarkson Potter: Lauren Monchik, Marysarah Quinn, Mark McCauslin, Joan Denman, Chloe Smith, and Barbara Marks. For a novice like me they were a revelation in efficiency, talent, and generosity of spirit.

For all my divine contributors, who made the book possible.

Support comes in various shapes and forms. A special thank you to all my friends who went through the labor pains with me. Get ready for second helpings.

And last, but always most, my husband Tommy Kempner, whose participation as my in-house editor and his enthusiasm and support for this book was limitless.

Contents

Introduction

My love affair with food goes back to my childhood days in San Francisco. I was the only child of only children and when my nanny tired of keeping me amused, she parked me in the kitchen. As it happened I enjoyed mixing, measuring, and licking bowls more than playing with dolls or on swing sets. And instead of reading fairy tales I read cookbooks. My favorite pastime was to read of fantastic desserts made with masses of eggs, butter, sugar, and chocolate. Somehow it was just as satisfying as eating them.

With that experience began a lifelong mania for collecting cookbooks as well as recipes from magazines and those of my mother's and grandmother's cooks. As a result of reading, watching, and helping our family cook—in other words by osmosis—I picked up a little knowledge and developed a love for haute cuisine.

I grew up in an era when young women took cooking classes before they married. So, fresh from college and before my marriage to Tommy Kempner, off I went. As I had a foundation, cooking school was really a way to fine-tune my skills, and I concentrated on learning to make the special things that I had drooled over in books. To this day, I still think my soufflés and pasta carbonara are as good as anyone's.

When Tommy and I moved to London for a year, right after we were married, I put my culinary skills to the test. Food was still rationed in 1952, and I realized that quality ingredients make a huge difference when you cook. In those days, I charmed a lot of butchers and greengrocers to get the extra lamb chop or a few more eggs. Rationing, however, did not prevent me from cooking up a storm, and oddly enough it's how I developed my lifelong love of entertaining. As is my nature, I made fast friends with a lot of people and soon I was inviting them to share in the weekly food packages we received from our parents, which were filled with delicacies like roast beef and tinned hams—things Londoners hadn't seen in years.

We lived in an eccentric little town house where the ill-equipped kitchen was in the basement and the dining room was on the first floor. I had to use a dumbwaiter to bring the food up and then rush to get it to the table before it became cold. I had my share of disasters due to a poor oven and a limited supply of pots and pans.

When we moved back to New York, and as a result of having three children in rapid succession, Sylvina Barrasso came into my life to be my cook and to my great good fortune has been with me—with one short intermission—for almost forty years.

Through the years, we've really experimented together. Sylvina is a natural and she can interpret any dish I've eaten in a restaurant or at a friend's house. Our menu planning has no formula; instead, we cook what we think our guests want to eat, which, of course, is what I want to eat at that particular moment. Along the way, we've adapted a wealth of recipes that I've collected and others we've invented ourselves.

For years, I've wanted to write a cookbook and share some of these recipes. When my fantasy came true, I realized that this book should include more than just my menus. I wanted to share with readers where I find my own inspiration to create new recipes and keep my food imaginative.

As it happens, the biggest influence comes from the memorable meals I've had all over the world

in some of the most beautiful houses belonging to my friends—lucky me. This book, however, is more than just a cookbook. In many ways, it's a memoir—a reflection of a part of my life that has given me extra pleasure not only because of the meals I've eaten with my friends, but also because of the way they entertain. My own style of entertaining has evolved from my happy experiences with the people I've profiled.

For the past four decades, in New York, I've given more dinner parties than I could possibly count. As a result, I'm often asked to impart my tips or secrets to great entertaining. I'm always stumped to give some brilliant quote. As for my menus, I have no formula for entertaining. Throwing a dinner or lunch party is a spontaneous happening that stems from a love of people and enjoyment of friends. For me, entertaining is part of the "living well is the best revenge" theory of life and gives me an opportunity to share what I do best. Offering good food and decorating with lovely flowers and pretty linens are ways of giving my friends happiness.

As a guest, what I notice as much as the food is presentation. Everything from the tablecloths to the way the food looks is as important as how the meal tastes. The last ingredient of successful entertaining and the one I prize above all others is the warmth of the host and the ambience he or she creates. You can have the best meal in the world, but without that personal touch, you may as well have gone to a four-star restaurant—not a dreary alternative, I know, but nothing in my view can compete with a well-executed dinner party at home.

Every menu illustrated in this book is highly personal and unpredictable. Nothing has been pre-fabricated for the camera, although in some instances I asked my host to re-create a favorite dish I'd had before. Best of all, the photographs vividly capture the way my friends live, and though I was on a professional mission, my visits were exactly like any other weekend, evening, or afternoon I've spent with them.

All these people have in common a generosity of spirit and friendship. For all of them, mealtime is happy time; the dining table is the place where friends meet to exchange ideas and relax. Though the majority of my friends have a cook and domestic help of some variety, they do not delegate the planning of their parties to staff. These hosts devote attention to every aspect of the event, from the menu to table settings to flowers to the ambience of the house.

Best of all, the food these people serve is food that's meant to be enjoyed and not just looked at. It's cooks' food as opposed to chefs' food. For me, that means straightforward, classically based cuisine. It's hearty; it's comforting and never fancy. Every recipe in this book can be executed by anyone.

This book offers a rare glimpse into the world I've been so fortunate to inhabit. In some instances, asking the hosts to participate in the book was my own sneaky way of getting them to part with recipes they've never given away. And so from the kitchens of my generous and skilled friends, I would like to share some of the better eating with you.

Ladies & GENTLEMEN

at
Lunch

Pastoral
Pursuits

WITH CATIE MARRON

If I believed in reincarnation, I would want to
come back as Catie and Don Marron's children. They
live in a big and little people's paradise. Imagine a
sprawling Victorian house that boasts an outdoor
playhouse, a topiary garden, a cutting garden, and a
kitchen garden, all situated overlooking a pond filled
with swans and ducks and just a few steps away from
the beach. That dreamy setting is the Marrons' country house in Southampton, New York.

Mrs. Donald Marron

CHILLED HERB AND LEAF SOUP

CRAB CAKES

SIMPLE SALAD WITH MUSTARD VINAIGRETTE

QUINOA SALAD

FRESH WATERMELON BALLS

OLD-FASHIONED
CHOCOLATE-CHIP COOKIES

COOK: MARIA McGRIFF

One of the things I love about New York is that socially there are few generational gaps. I have friends of all ages. Catie is one of my young friends. She's tall, thin, and a classic American beauty. Her houses and her food are as pretty as she is. In her professional life, she was an executive on Wall Street, where she met Don, the chairman of PaineWebber. After a stint at *Vogue,* her focus is now on raising her children and running her household. And she puts as much thought and intelligence into that as she did her career. For me, Catie is a homemaker in the best sense of the word. She loves all the details.

It takes a long time for someone who entertains to create a personal signature, but Catie has come into her own much sooner than most. Our lunch was in the garden and it had all the right elements for a summer meal. Chilled herb and leaf soup—made with ingredients right out of her garden—was a cool start to an imaginative combination of crab cakes and quinoa salad. The blend of the classic and the unusual is a feature of her menus. Quite often grain-based salads can taste so healthy that they're bland, but Catie solved that problem by sautéing the vegetables, tossing in prosciutto, and then adding that great elixir, mayonnaise, to quinoa, something I'd never had before. For dessert it was chocolate-chip cookies, a mainstay of any household with children. This menu was as it should be: reflective of the woman who created it. In this case that means modern, up-to-date, and youthful.

Chilled Herb and Leaf Soup

SERVES 4

1 shallot, peeled
1 cup fresh flat-leaf parsley leaves
2 cups torn butterhead lettuce leaves
2 cups torn spinach leaves
2 tablespoons fresh lemon juice
1 ripe avocado, peeled, pitted, and cut into chunks
3 tablespoons cold cream cheese
2 cups chicken stock, chilled
Salt
¼ cup finely chopped fresh chives, for garnish
Freshly ground black pepper
2 tablespoons softened cream cheese, beaten with a fork until smooth (optional)

Place the shallot and parsley in the bowl of a food processor and process until finely minced. Add the lettuce, spinach, and lemon juice and process until finely chopped and combined. Add the avocado and the 3 tablespoons of cream cheese and process until smooth.

With the motor running at low speed, gradually add the chilled chicken stock. Continue to process until the soup is well blended. Season with salt and chill until ready to serve.

To serve, divide the soup among 4 soup bowls and garnish with the chopped chives, pepper, and a swirl of cream cheese, if desired.

Crab Cakes

SERVES 4

5 slices firm white bread, crusts removed
1 cup whole milk
1 pound lump crabmeat, picked over to remove any shell
½ cup mayonnaise
⅓ cup finely chopped fresh cilantro leaves
⅓ cup finely chopped fresh dill
¼ cup finely chopped fresh flat-leaf parsley
Juice of ½ lemon
1 small red onion, finely chopped
Salt and freshly ground black pepper
Vegetable oil for frying
½ cup unbleached all-purpose flour
2 large eggs, beaten
¾ cup dry bread crumbs

In a medium bowl, soak the bread slices in the milk for 5 to 10 minutes. Squeeze out any excess milk and crumble the bread back into the bowl. Add the crabmeat, mayonnaise, cilantro, dill, parsley, lemon juice, and onion. Mix thoroughly with a wooden spoon, season with salt and pepper, and allow the mixture to rest in the refrigerator for 30 minutes.

Shape the mixture into 4-inch patties using your hands. The mixture should make about 6 patties. Line a plate with a paper towel and place the patties on the plate to rest.

In a hot, large, heavy frying pan, pour in enough vegetable oil to reach about a quarter of the way up the sides of the pan. Heat the oil to 300°F.

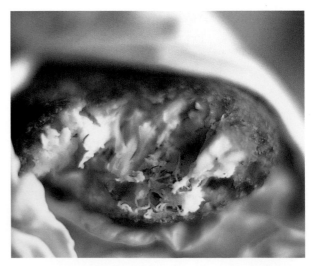

Place the flour, beaten eggs, and bread crumbs in 3 shallow bowls. When the oil is hot, dip each of the patties first in the flour, then in the beaten eggs, and then in the bread crumbs. Fry the crab cakes for 3 minutes on each side, until golden brown and crispy. Drain on paper towels and serve hot.

Simple Salad with Mustard Vinaigrette

SERVES 4

2 teaspoons Dijon mustard
4 teaspoons extra-virgin olive oil
1 teaspoon white vinegar
¼ teaspoon dark brown sugar
Pinch of salt
Freshly ground white pepper to taste
2 heads of butterhead lettuce, stems removed, washed, dried, and torn
3 chopped scallions (white parts only)
1 English cucumber, peeled and diced

In a spouted measuring cup, combine the mustard, oil, vinegar, brown sugar, and salt and whisk until smooth. Season with white pepper.

Place the torn lettuce, scallions, and diced cucumber in a medium salad bowl. Pour on the mustard vinaigrette and toss well.

Quinoa Salad

Quinoa was a staple of the ancient Incas, who called it the "mother grain." Hailed as the super-grain of the future, it contains more protein than any other grain. This salad is delicious served warm or cold.

SERVES 4

1 cup quinoa
Salt to taste
2 tablespoons unsalted butter
¼ cup extra-virgin olive oil
1 cup finely chopped scallions (white and green parts)
2 cups diced yellow zucchini

2 cups diced green zucchini
2 cups peeled, seeded, and diced tomatoes
¼ cup finely chopped fresh flat-leaf parsley
1 tablespoon mayonnaise
¼ cup chopped prosciutto (optional)
Freshly ground black pepper to taste

Place the quinoa in a saucepan with 2 cups of water and a pinch of salt. Over high heat bring to a boil, reduce the heat to low, and simmer, covered with a tight-fitting lid, for 15 minutes, until the water is absorbed. Set aside.

In a large skillet, melt the butter with the olive oil over medium heat. Add the scallions and zucchini and sauté for 5 minutes, until the scallions are slightly translucent. Remove from the heat and stir in the tomatoes, parsley, mayonnaise, and prosciutto. Season with salt and pepper.

In a large serving bowl, thoroughly combine the vegetable mixture with the cooked quinoa. Serve.

Old-Fashioned Chocolate-Chip Cookies

Catie serves an assortment of cookies, including rich shortbreads and these nostalgically sweet and simple chocolate-studded favorites, with cooling fresh melon for a light, ladylike dessert.

MAKES 2 DOZEN

¾ cup unbleached all-purpose flour
½ teaspoon baking soda
Pinch of salt
½ cup (1 stick) unsalted butter, at room temperature
¾ cup packed light brown sugar
½ teaspoon vanilla extract
1 large egg
½ cup quick-cooking oats (not instant)
1 cup semisweet chocolate morsels (or broken pieces of a semisweet chocolate block)

Preheat the oven to 375°F. Lightly grease 2 baking sheets.

In a medium mixing bowl, sift together the flour, baking soda, and salt. In another medium bowl, combine the butter, brown sugar, and vanilla and beat until light and fluffy. Beat in the egg. Slowly add the flour mixture, beating after each addition. Beat until smooth. Stir in the oats. Gently fold in the chocolate morsels until they are evenly incorporated.

Drop the cookie batter by rounded tablespoonfuls, 3 inches apart, onto the prepared baking sheets. Bake for 9 minutes, or until golden. Remove from the oven and transfer the cookies to a wire rack to cool.

Her **surroundings** and her food are as **pretty** as she is.

Lunch in Deauville

WITH ANNE D'ORNANO

Anne d'Ornano happens to be one of the few really important people I know. Since 1977, she has been the mayor of Deauville, France. And that's only one of her positions. Her husband, Michel, a former minister of culture under Valéry Giscard d'Estaing, was also the counsel general of Trouville and the President of the General Council of Calvados. After his death, in 1991, Anne succeeded him as counsel general in both towns. Her other community interests are numerous and it was Anne who founded, along with Jack Valenti, the Deauville Film Festival. Along the way, she received the Chevalier de la Légion d'Honneur in 1986, and nine years later she was awarded the title of l'Officier de la Légion d'Honneur.

Countess Anne d'Ornano

SCALLOP SALAD

STUFFED TOMATOES

POACHED TURBOT WITH
BEURRE BLANC

TARTE TATIN

Her house in Deauville was built not long ago, but you would never know it; it's designed in the traditional Normandy style with arched windows, shingled mansard roof, and white bricks. Lush meadows, fields, and apple orchards surround the house. And as it's set high on a hill, there's a commanding view of Deauville and the English Channel beyond.

Anne has had several different cooks over the years, and they've always been superb. Our menu was deliciously regional. Normandy is renowned for its seafood, so we started with a seafood salad followed by turbot. As apples are indigenous, the meal was finished off with a classic tarte Tatin. Our first two courses were washed down with local rosé. Years ago, Anne introduced me to the habit of drinking rosé, which seems to be another Norman favorite and the d'Ornano house drink.

Anne has so many official dinners, lunches, and meetings that she rarely entertains at home. When she has the opportunity, she prefers small groups of close friends. She likes to keep it as simple as possible, so for even a small number the main course is served buffet-style.

In addition to her time-consuming professional life, Anne is a devoted mother and grandmother, and she also runs two other houses—one in Paris and another in Provence—with minimal staff. When I visit her, I always marvel at how effortlessly she manages to juggle all her roles.

Yet despite her hectic schedule, she's so relaxed when she entertains that her guests also feel at ease. She understands creature comforts and surrounds you with comfort as well—you never want to leave the guest rooms. It's more than the fact that her house is fabulous and her food is delicious, though; the predominant feature of a weekend or dinner with Anne is the warmth and affection she has for friends.

Scallop Salad

SERVES 6

2 pounds sea scallops
1½ cups white wine, such as Chardonnay
24 large shrimp, peeled and deveined
3 tablespoons raspberry vinegar
½ cup light olive oil
2 shallots, very thinly sliced into rounds
Salt and freshly ground black pepper to taste
1 bunch of endive, washed and torn into thin
    strips
5 large eggs, boiled and halved
2 cups cherry tomatoes, halved

Remove any roe from the scallops and pull off
the tough side muscles.

In a large frying pan, bring the white wine to a
simmer over medium heat. Reduce the heat, add
the scallops and shrimp, and simmer for 3 minutes, until the scallops are just cooked through.
Remove the scallops and shrimp with a slotted
spoon and set aside. Discard the cooking liquid.

Place the vinegar in a medium bowl and,
whisking constantly, add the olive oil so that the
mixture emulsifies. Add the shallots and salt and
pepper.

Combine the scallops and shrimp with the
endive in a large bowl. Pour the vinaigrette over
the seafood, tossing gently until evenly coated.
Pile the salad onto a large serving platter, garnish
with the halved eggs and cherry tomatoes, and
serve immediately.

Stuffed Tomatoes

SERVES 6

6 medium, firm ripe tomatoes
Salt and freshly ground black pepper to taste
3 cups smoked ham (about 12 ounces), finely
    chopped
2 shallots, minced
1 bunch of curly parsley, roughly chopped
    (about 1 cup)
1 tablespoon salted butter, softened

Preheat the oven to 350°F. Lightly grease a baking sheet with olive oil or butter.

Carefully cut a ¼-inch slice off the top of each
tomato. Using a teaspoon, scoop out the seeds
and core from each tomato and discard.
Generously sprinkle the inside of each hollowed-
out tomato with salt. Place the tomatoes on the
baking sheet and set aside.

In a large bowl, combine the ham, shallots,
parsley, and butter. Season with salt and pepper.
Loosely fill each tomato to the top with the ham
mixture, mounding slightly. Bake for 30 minutes,
or until the mixture is bubbling and the tomatoes
are tender. Serve immediately.

Poached Turbot

*Turbot is a highly prized European flatfish with
firm, lean, white flesh and a deliciously mild flavor.
Flounder may be substituted.*

SERVES 6

4 quarts Court Bouillon (recipe follows)
3 sprigs of fresh thyme
2 fresh bay leaves
4 sprigs of fresh flat-leaf parsley
1 lemon, thinly sliced into rounds
¼ teaspoon fennel seeds (optional)
1 turbot, about 4 to 6 pounds, cleaned
2 tablespoons olive oil
Salt and freshly ground black pepper to taste
Beurre Blanc (recipe follows)

Pour 4 cups of the court bouillon into a large
roasting pan that will hold the whole fish. Add
the thyme, bay leaves, parsley, lemon slices, and

fennel seeds if using. Brush the fish with the oil, and season with salt and pepper. Place the turbot into the pan white side down and add enough of the remaining court bouillon to completely cover the fish.

Place the pan on the stovetop (you may need to use 2 burners) and bring the liquid to a simmer. As soon as the liquid begins to bubble, reduce the heat to low and simmer for 7 minutes per pound of fish, or until the fish flakes at the bone when tested with a fork through the thickest part. Using 2 large spatulas, carefully remove the fish from the liquid to a large, warmed platter. Remove the skin and any dark flesh and serve immediately with the Beurre Blanc.

COURT BOUILLON
MAKES 4 QUARTS

2 large carrots, peeled and chopped
4 celery stalks, chopped
2 medium onions, chopped
6 sprigs of fresh thyme
2 large sprigs of fresh flat-leaf parsley
4 quarts water
1 quart dry white wine
4 teaspoons salt
8 black peppercorns

Combine all the ingredients in a large saucepan over high heat. Bring the mixture to a boil, reduce the heat to medium-low, and simmer for 40 minutes. Strain the mixture through a fine sieve into a large bowl and discard the solids.

BEURRE BLANC

*This classic French sauce is composed of a wine, vinegar, and shallot reduction.
It's delicious served with fish or poultry.*

SERVES 6

2 cups (4 sticks) unsalted butter,
    cut into small pieces
4 shallots, finely chopped
½ cup white wine vinegar
½ cup dry white wine
2 tablespoons crème fraîche
Salt and freshly ground black pepper to taste

In a heavy, medium saucepan, melt 1 tablespoon of the butter over medium heat. Add the shallots, white wine vinegar, and white wine and bring to a simmer. Simmer for 7 minutes, until the shallots are tender.

Just before serving, strain the wine mixture through a fine metal sieve into a clean, heavy, medium saucepan, pressing the shallots to extract as much liquid as possible.

Place the saucepan over low heat, return to a simmer, and whisk in the remaining pieces of butter, whisking well between additions so that each piece of butter has melted before adding the next. Do not allow the sauce to boil at any point or it may separate. Stir in the crème fraîche, season with salt and pepper, and serve immediately.

Tarte Tatin

The French call this famed tart "tarte des demoiselles Tatin," the tart of two unmarried sisters named Tatin. Its delicious caramel topping is exposed when the tart is inverted onto a serving plate.

SERVES 6

½ lemon
5 apples, such as Granny Smith or Golden Delicious
½ cup (1 stick) unsalted butter, cut into small pieces
½ cup plus 4 tablespoons sugar
Pâte Brisée (recipe follows)

Preheat the oven to 400°F.

Fill a large bowl with water and squeeze the lemon half into the water. Peel the apples and cut into quarters. Remove the cores and slice each quarter thinly. Place the slices in the acidulated water and set aside.

Grease a heavy, 8-inch-round, 3-inch-deep baking pan with 2 tablespoons of the butter. Sprinkle 2 tablespoons of the sugar over the bottom and sides of the pan. Arrange a layer of drained apple slices decoratively in the bottom of the pan. Sprinkle with one third of the ½ cup of sugar and dot with one third of the butter. Repeat the layering until all the apples, the rest of the ½ cup of sugar, and the butter are used.

On a lightly floured surface, roll out the pastry to a disk ⅛-inch thick and 10 inches in diameter, so that the pastry fits over the apples with a 1-inch overhang. Tuck the overhanging pastry down the sides of the apples.

Bake the tart on the lowest rack in the oven for 40 minutes, or until the pastry is golden on top and the apples are tender when tested with a skewer. Remove from the oven and allow to cool for 5 minutes before inverting onto a large baking sheet.

Preheat the broiler. Sprinkle the remaining 2 tablespoons of sugar evenly over the cooked apples and broil the tart for 5 minutes, or until the sugar has caramelized and is bubbling. Slide the tart onto a serving plate and serve warm, in slices.

PÂTE BRISÉE

This is the classic French pastry for pies or tarts. The dough may be made ahead and frozen for up to one month.

MAKES TWO 9-INCH CRUSTS

2½ cups all-purpose flour
1 teaspoon salt
1 teaspoon sugar
1 cup (2 sticks) unsalted butter, chilled and cut into small pieces
¼ cup ice water

In the bowl of a food processor, combine the flour, salt, and sugar. Add the butter and process until the mixture resembles coarse meal, about 10 seconds.

With the machine running, add the ice water in a slow, steady stream. Pulse until the dough holds together without being sticky, being careful not to process for more than 30 seconds. To test when the pastry is ready, pinch a small amount together. If it is crumbly add more ice water, 1 teaspoon at a time.

Divide the dough into 2 equal balls, flatten slightly into disks, and wrap in plastic. Place in the refrigerator and chill for at least 1 hour before use.

FRESH FLOWERS ADORN EVERY ROOM IN ANNE'S HOUSE.

FINGER BOWLS WITH LEMON ARE A NICE TOUCH.

THE FAVORITE SPOT OF MADLY, ANNA'S DACHSHUND.

BOXWOODS LINE THE FRONT WALK.

ABOVE: ANNE'S TABLE SHOWCASES HER WARM STYLE. BELOW: THE TOMATOES READY FOR STUFFING.

HOME IS WHERE THE HEARTH IS.

The predominant feature of a weekend or dinner with Anne is the warmth and affection she has for friends.

Light Fare

WITH PRINCESS MARIE-CHANTAL

Marie-Chantal is one of my younger friends. Four years ago she married Prince Pavlos of Greece, whom I've known since he was a small child. They are now the parents of a three-year-old daughter and a son who was six months at the time of our lunch.

Marie-Chantal and her friends are busy, modern women who, after spending time with their children, have little time for girls' lunches. She's solved the problem, however, by entertaining at home, so that her friends can bring their children. "It's difficult in New York to find a restaurant that's suitable for my

Crown Princess Pavlos of Greece

GRAPEFRUIT GAZPACHO WITH MINT

CORN AND FETA SOUFFLÉ

INDIVIDUAL LEMON TARTS

CHEF: PATRICK GARDÈRE

friends and me to go to with our kids. They're either too formal or too crowded, plus the children become restless."

For this lunch Marie Chantal invited five friends, all of whom are in their mid- to late twenties, and their children, who were under the age of five; her sister Alex even brought her seventeen-day-old son. Some of the other mothers had recently had babies, and naturally they were conscious of their weight. With that in mind, Marie-Chantal chose a spa menu. This type of cuisine was a first for me. The food was so tasty and fulfilling that I'm still baffled as to how the chef, Patrick Gardère, can create a corn and feta soufflé without adding flour that has only two grams of fat.

Marie-Chantal grew up in Hong Kong and her table decoration was Asian-inspired. Instead of a floral center-piece, miniature blue-and-white Chinese porcelain vases filled with pale pink sweet peas were scattered around the table. Silver plates were used as liners for the blue-and-white china that complemented the porcelain. The white linen place mats and napkins looked particularly crisp with the Asian tableware.

The children dined on spaghetti with tomato sauce at their own little table. Children and sauce are always an accident waiting to happen, but Marie-Chantal didn't opt for practicality. She gave her tiny guests equal treatment and set their table with a lovely linen tablecloth and matching napkins. The centerpiece was the same as ours.

"Sweet peas for our sweet peas," said Marie-Chantal. She's now at work on illustrations for a possible children's book about a magic frog.

Marie-Chantal's gathering was a trip down memory lane for me. It's been nearly forty years since I've been to a luncheon party with a group of women who are mothers of small children. In my day, however, we didn't bring the children to lunch. But the conversation was still centered on the same topics: child rearing, schooling, and family holidays. In this age of casual convenience, it was refreshing to see Marie-Chantal create an afternoon with children that had the refinement of a former era when manners and tradition were second nature.

Grapefruit Gazpacho with Mint

This tangy soup is perfect for a light summer luncheon, served chilled and garnished with tiny dice of cucumber, radish, mint, and tomato.

SERVES 6

1 cucumber, peeled, seeded, and finely diced
2 tomatoes, cored and finely diced
½ cup finely diced celery
½ cup finely diced red bell pepper
3 scallions (white and green parts), finely diced
1½ cups fresh grapefruit juice
2 tablespoons chopped fresh mint
2 tablespoons chopped fresh flat-leaf parsley

Reserve 1 tablespoon each of finely diced cucumber, tomato, celery, bell pepper, and scallions from the vegetable mixture.

In a large bowl, combine the grapefruit juice with the remaining cucumber, tomatoes, celery, bell pepper, and scallions and the mint and parsley. Mix well, cover, and refrigerate for 1 hour to blend the flavors.

Working in batches, transfer the chilled soup to the bowl of a food processor fitted with a steel blade, and purée until smooth. Divide the soup among 6 soup bowls and garnish with the diced vegetables.

Corn and Feta Soufflé

Fresh corn is always a treat and combined with the feta it makes an especially flavorful low-fat dish.

SERVES 6

½ teaspoon olive oil
1 shallot, minced
1 red bell pepper, stemmed, seeded, and diced
1 garlic clove, minced
2 tablespoons chopped fresh oregano
2 tablespoons chopped fresh basil
½ teaspoon freshly ground black pepper, plus more to taste
3 cups fresh corn kernels cut from the cob (about 6 ears)
1 medium potato, peeled and grated
2 large egg yolks, lightly beaten
1 tablespoon unbleached all-purpose flour
¾ cup low-fat cottage cheese
2 tablespoons crumbled feta cheese
2 tablespoons grated low-fat mozzarella cheese
Salt
6 large egg whites at room temperature

Preheat the oven to 425°F.

Heat the olive oil in a large sauté pan over medium heat. Add the shallot, bell pepper, garlic, oregano, basil, black pepper, corn, and potato and sauté for 10 to 12 minutes, until the corn is cooked through. Transfer half of the mixture to a food processor and purée. Transfer the puréed mixture together with the sautéed mixture to a large bowl and stir to combine. Add the egg yolks, flour, cottage cheese, feta, and mozzarella and mix well. Season with salt and pepper.

Combine the egg whites and a pinch of salt in a large mixing bowl and beat until stiff peaks form. Gently fold the whites into the corn mixture until just combined. Pour the soufflé mixture into two 8-inch soufflé dishes and bake for about 40 minutes, until set.

Individual Lemon Tarts

These individual tarts are made without pastry crusts, cutting their fat content way down. It's a no-guilt sweet treat to complete this healthful lunch.

MAKES 6 TARTS

4 egg yolks, beaten
1 cup sugar
3 tablespoons fresh lemon juice
1 tablespoon finely grated lemon zest
½ cup fresh orange juice
1 cup heavy cream
Confectioners' sugar, for dusting

Preheat the oven to 375°F.

In a medium bowl, whisk the egg yolks and the sugar together until light and fluffy. Add the lemon juice, zest, and orange juice and stir to combine.

Pour the cream into a medium saucepan and bring to a boil over medium heat. Immediately remove from the heat and allow to cool for 5 minutes. Pour the cream into the egg mixture and whisk to combine, then pour through a fine sieve. Pour the mixture into individual 2-inch muffin molds and bake for 10 minutes, until set. Allow to cool for 10 minutes before serving.

To serve, unmold from the tin onto 6 dessert plates and dust with confectioners' sugar.

"Sweet peas for our sweet peas."

In Betsy's Garden

When Betsy Bloomingdale enters a
room everyone notices. It's understandable. She's
tall, great-looking, and exquisitely dressed. But it's
more than just those qualities that sends a hush over
a room. Betsy exudes a warmth and good humor that
is instantly contagious to all those who come into
her orbit.

   Betsy is the widow of Alfred Bloomingdale, who
was the founder of Diner's Club. She was born and
bred in Los Angeles, where she still lives and is happily surrounded by her three grown children and
eight grandchildren. Betsy traveled extensively with

Mrs. Alfred Bloomingdale

CHILLED BEET SOUP WITH
CRÈME FRAÎCHE AND CAVIAR

CHICKEN MOUSSE WITH AVOCADO
SAUCE AND RED PEPPER SAUCE

STRAWBERRIES WITH
CANDIED CITRUS ZEST

LINDA'S SECRET ORANGE CAKE

COOK: ERLINDA DE LAS ARMAS

Nancy Reagan when she was First Lady. But long before the Reagans became the First Family, Betsy was renowned on both coasts for her sense of style and her philanthropic efforts. She serves on the board of the Friends of Art and Preservation for American Embassies. She's also a founding member of the James Madison Council for the Library of Congress. In Los Angeles, Betsy's principal charity is The Colleagues, which supports the Children's International Institute for Abused Children.

Like all my afternoons and evenings at Betsy's house, our lunch was memorable. It was a rare California summer day—not oppressively hot, as it can be at that time of year, but clear and sunny with a warm, gentle breeze grazing the air. The garden was in full bloom and the view from the atrium was a sea of eye-popping color. The table was brimming with imaginative food, homegrown flowers, and lively conversation.

The luncheon was ladylike but satisfying. "I've discovered," observes Betsy, "that people for the most part like wonderful, simple food." Her menus vary according to the time of day and season. Our summer lunch was a light combination of chilled beet soup followed by a cold chicken mousse served with a choice of sauces. In winter, she's found that her short ribs and mashed potato recipes are big hits with her guests. She likes to balance such hearty, homey fare with a more extravagant first course. For our lunch, the beet soup included crème fraîche and caviar. "For a main course like short ribs, I'd do something like smoked salmon and caviar to start," she explains.

What has always struck me about her style of entertaining is her eye for colorful detail. One of the great joys of Betsy's life is gardening. Her fabulous flower gardens are the springboard for her choice of table setting. She selects from among her many sets of china according to which flowers are in season. Clivia, for example, looks wonderful with her antique Crown Derby service. The huge dahlias of summer are dazzling against the informal and colorful Faience dishes that she uses for more informal dining. And the wide variety of roses that bloom in her garden from late March through December look sensational with everything.

Like all great hostesses, Betsy artfully manages to make her parties look effortless. Her motto is a simple one: Enjoy yourself. If you don't, your guests won't either. "When the first guest arrives," she told me, "I go to my own party." But Betsy's parties are never about Betsy. She likes to have a reason for inviting her guests, so she plans them around a guest of honor and invites guests the honored one would like to meet or has asked to have included. In the end, Betsy's philosophy on entertaining is really a reflection of her generous spirit. "I hope that when I entertain," she told me, "it comes off as warm, delicious, elegant, and fun."

Chilled Beet Soup with Crème Fraîche and Caviar

If you are pressed for time, feel free to substitute two 15-ounce cans of baby beets for the roasted beets.

SERVES 4

2 pounds beets, trimmed
2 14-ounce cans chicken broth
1 tablespoon dry sherry
Juice of 1 lemon
¼ cup crème fraîche, for garnish
4 tablespoons black caviar, for garnish

Preheat the oven to 350°F. Wrap the beets individually in foil and bake in the oven for 1 hour, or until they can be easily pierced with a knife tip. Let cool, then slip off the skins and quarter.

Place the beets in the bowl of a food processor and purée until smooth. Add the broth, sherry, and lemon juice and blend until well combined.

Pour the soup into a large bowl, cover, and chill for 1 hour. When the soup is ready to serve, divide among 4 bowls and garnish with a dollop of crème fraîche and a tablespoon of caviar.

Chicken Mousse

This dish can be made a few days ahead and kept in the refrigerator until serving time. Betsy served it with aspic and endive leaves.

SERVES 8

4 boneless, skinless chicken breasts, cubed
2 large eggs
½ cup heavy cream
½ teaspoon salt
Dash of white pepper
Dash of Tabasco sauce
1 tablespoon salted butter
1 small shallot, minced
2 tablespoons minced red bell pepper
½ cup chopped pistachios
Avocado Sauce (recipe follows)
Red Pepper Sauce (recipe follows)

Preheat the oven to 350°F.

Place the cubed chicken in the bowl of a food processor and process until very finely chopped. Add the eggs, one at a time, processing between additions. With the motor running slowly, add the heavy cream. Add the salt, white pepper, and Tabasco sauce and process until combined. Transfer the mixture to a medium mixing bowl, cover, and set aside.

In a medium sauté pan, melt the butter over medium heat. When the butter sizzles, add the shallot and red pepper and cook, stirring, until tender, 5 to 6 minutes. Stir the cooked shallot and red pepper and the pistachios into the chicken mixture.

Spread a 16-inch length of plastic wrap on a flat surface. Spoon the chicken mixture in a 12-inch strip along the center of the plastic. Shape the chicken mixture into a roll and wrap firmly in the plastic, twisting the ends to seal. Wrap the roll in foil and twist the ends firmly.

Place the chicken roll in a 10 × 14 × 3-inch baking dish and pour in enough hot water to come halfway up the sides of the roll. Bake for approximately 45 minutes, or until the roll feels firm and is cooked through when tested with a metal skewer.

Remove the roll to a platter to cool. When cool enough to handle, remove the foil and refrigerate, still in the plastic wrap, until completely chilled, about 3 hours. To serve, remove the roll from the refrigerator. Remove the plastic and cut the mousse into ½-inch slices. Serve with the avocado and red pepper sauces.

AVOCADO SAUCE
MAKES 1 CUP

¼ cup fresh cilantro leaves
3 small or 1 large ripe avocado, peeled and cut
    into chunks
¼ cup mayonnaise
2 tablespoons fresh lime juice
Dash of Tabasco sauce
Dash of salt
Dash of white pepper

In the bowl of a food processor, process the cilantro until finely chopped. Add the avocado, mayonnaise, lime juice, Tabasco sauce, salt, and white pepper and process until smooth. If the sauce appears too thick, slowly add 1 to 2 tablespoons of water, processing until the sauce reaches a yogurt-like consistency. Transfer to a small bowl, cover, and refrigerate until ready to serve.

RED PEPPER SAUCE
MAKES ¾ CUP

2 red bell peppers
2 teaspoons balsamic vinegar
1 teaspoon sugar
⅛ teaspoon minced garlic
Dash of salt
Dash of white pepper

Preheat a broiler pan in the broiler. Place the peppers on the pan and broil, using tongs to turn, until the peppers are charred on all sides. Remove the peppers from the broiler and place at once in a plastic bag. Seal tightly and let stand for 10 minutes to allow the skins to steam loose. When cooled, remove the skins, stems, and seeds.

In the bowl of a food processor, combine the roasted peppers with the vinegar, sugar, garlic, salt, and white pepper. Process until the mixture is smooth. Transfer to a small bowl, cover, and refrigerate until ready to serve.

Strawberries with Candied Citrus Zest

These are delicious served on their own or with a simple cake. The aromatic oils in the citrus zest add a perfumed essence to the berries.

SERVES 4

2 pints strawberries, washed and stems removed

RIND SAUCE
Zest of 2 oranges, cut into julienne
Zest of 2 lemons, cut into julienne
Zest of 1 lime, cut into julienne
2 cups sugar
½ teaspoon cream of tartar

Place the strawberries in a large serving bowl. Bring a medium saucepan of water to a boil. Blanch the combined zests for 1 to 2 minutes, until just tender. Strain into a sieve and refresh the zests by running under cold water. Drain thoroughly and set aside.

In a medium saucepan, combine the sugar with 1 cup of water and the cream of tartar. Stir over medium heat to dissolve the sugar. Bring the liquid to a boil, add the zests, reduce the heat, and simmer for 15 minutes, or until the zests are translucent.

Remove from the heat and cool for 10 to 15 minutes. Pour over the strawberries and allow to stand for 1 hour before serving.

Linda's Secret Orange Cake

This light and fluffy cake is perfect for dessert or for afternoon tea.

SERVES 8

1½ cups granulated sugar
1¼ cups sifted all-purpose flour
¼ cup fresh orange juice
Grated zest of 2 oranges
7 large egg yolks
8 large egg whites
1 teaspoon salt
½ teaspoon cream of tartar
3 tablespoons confectioners' sugar, for dusting

Preheat the oven to 350°F.

Grease only the bottom of a 10-inch tube pan. Line the bottom with wax paper and grease lightly.

Sift ½ cup of the sugar together with the flour four times into a medium mixing bowl.

In another medium mixing bowl, beat together the orange juice and zest and the remaining 1 cup of sugar. Add the egg yolks and continue to beat until light in color, about 3 minutes. Add the flour mixture 2 tablespoons at a time, beating until smooth after each addition.

Place the egg whites and salt in a large mixing bowl and beat until frothy. Add the cream of tartar and beat until stiff peaks form.

Spoon one third of the egg whites into the batter and mix well with a clean wooden spoon. Using a rubber spatula, gently fold in the remaining egg whites.

Pour half of the batter into the prepared pan and use a rubber spatula to level. Pour in the remaining batter and level again. Lightly tap the pan on the counter 3 times to release air pockets.

Bake for 50 to 60 minutes, until a skewer inserted in the center comes out clean and the cake springs back when lightly pressed. Invert the pan immediately onto a wine bottle; cool the cake completely in the pan.

Turn the cake right side up and loosen the sides and the center core with a thin sharp knife, avoiding any up-and-down motions. Invert onto a serving plate and sprinkle with sifted confectioners' sugar. Cut with a sharp knife dipped in water.

"People for the most part like wonderful, simple food."

Lively Luncheon
with London's
Best

If Marguerite Littman's house on Chester Square in London could speak, it would spin enchanting tales of true American southern hospitality. Since 1965, the New Orleans–born southern belle has been giving her famous lunches and dinners, assembling a glamorous coterie of people who range from the world of the arts to high finance to the British aristocracy. The list of people who have dined at Chester Square reads like a veritable Who's Who: Elizabeth Taylor, David Hockney, and the late Princess of Wales, to name a few. When out-of-town friends arrive in London, Marguerite is the first person they call, and she's always at the ready to arrange a lunch with people they might never meet otherwise.

Mr. and Mrs. Mark Littman

LOBSTER WITH MANGO, PAPAYA,
AND MELON

CURRIED APRICOT MAYONNAISE

"BARBECUED" SPRING LAMB WITH
ROSEMARY

SAUTÉED BANANAS

STUFFED BAKED POTATOES

FRESH ENGLISH GARDEN PEAS

APPLE SORBET WITH CALVADOS AND
GINGER

FRESH RASPBERRY PURÉE

COOK: VICTOR BECKFORD

Stimulating conversation abounds and not just from her illustrious guests. Her English husband, Mark Littman, is a barrister and Queen's Counselor who regales the guests with fascinating stories. And Marguerite shares her anecdotes of a life well lived. It was she who coached Elizabeth Taylor to "speak southern" for the film *Cat on a Hot Tin Roof,* and her friendships with everyone from Tennessee Williams to Igor Stravinsky have given her a wealth of stories.

Marguerite's gatherings are usually luncheons for the simple reason that she has more energy to pamper her guests in the middle of the day. "I like my parties to have a beginning, a middle, and an end," she told me, "so guests can get up from the table and go when they feel like it. At the end of a dinner party I think guests wonder how long they must stay over a brandy upstairs in the drawing room. I don't mind eat-and-run guests." Her dazzling guest lists belie a casual nature; Marguerite rarely asks people more than two or three days in advance, and she prefers eight to ten people at the most.

I've never been to Marguerite's when anything from food to wine to flowers was less than impeccable, but she's had her share of mishaps over the years. The legendary Lady Diana Cooper's dog once ate the top off a cheese soufflé, and on another occasion chocolate pots de crème came out as chocolate soup. Her guest, Andy Warhol, cheerfully announced that hot chocolate soup was the only dessert he liked.

For me, Marguerite's house is one of the best places to eat in London. She's a stickler for fresh food,

and seasonal cooking is high on her list of priorities as well; you're apt to get the freshest of anything first at Marguerite's. Her menus are always full of surprises. After all her years in England, her food still has a southern accent to it. Creole dishes are frequently served up and mingle happily with more expected fare. Fillet of sole might be served with ginger. Southern fried chicken is followed by a prune soufflé. For our lunch, a first course of lobster with mango, papaya, and melon was served with an Anglo-Indian curried apricot mayonnaise. Rack of spring lamb, a traditional English favorite, was marinated in a classic southern barbecue sauce. To accompany the lamb she served a blend of the classic and the exotic. One of her signature dishes, stuffed baked potatoes, found itself sharing a plate with sautéed bananas and fresh English garden peas that were spruced up with mint and sugar. Blackberries and apple are two fruits you rarely see used for sorbet. These inventive combinations are as magical as Marguerite herself.

Though Truman Capote was said to have modeled his southern heroine Holly Golightly after her, Marguerite is the farthest thing from frivolous or flighty. Fourteen years ago she leveraged her social position into something more substantial than lunch and founded the AIDS Crisis Trust in England. Her famous lunches may be a platform on which to indulge her wit and playfulness, but her tireless work for this cause has ultimately given her the role for which she is now best known.

the lobster tails off the bodies. With a mallet, crack the claws and remove the claw meat; place it in a medium bowl. Use a sharp, heavy knife to cut the tail in half lengthwise, remove the meat, and cut it into chunks. Add the tail meat to the bowl of claw meat, reserving the tail shells for serving. Cover the lobster meat and refrigerate until ready to serve.

To serve, fill each of the halved lobster shells with the chunks of meat and arrange on a platter with slices of the mango, papaya, and melon and wedges of lemon and lime. Serve the lobster with the mayonnaise.

Curried Apricot Mayonnaise

MAKES 1 CUP

2 large egg yolks
1 teaspoon curry powder
Cayenne pepper to taste
2 tablespoons apricot jelly, pressed through a fine
  sieve
Juice of 1 lemon
¼ cup light olive oil
¼ cup walnut oil
Salt and white pepper to taste

Place the egg yolks, curry powder, cayenne, apricot jelly, and lemon juice in the bowl of a food processor and process to combine. Combine the olive and walnut oils in a measuring cup and, with the motor running, add the oils to the yolk mixture in a thin, steady stream. The mixture will thicken and emulsify. Season with salt and white pepper to taste.

Spoon the mayonnaise into a sauce boat, cover, and refrigerate until ready to serve.

Lobster with Mango, Papaya, and Melon

The sweet, succulent flavors of the lobster and fruits are given just a hint of southern spice when served with Victor's special curried apricot mayonnaise.

SERVES 6

3 small live lobsters (about 1 pound each)
1 ripe medium mango, peeled and sliced
1 medium papaya, peeled, seeded, and sliced
1 honeydew melon or cantaloupe, peeled, seeded,
  and sliced
1 lemon, sliced into thin wedges
1 lime, sliced into thin wedges
Curried Apricot Mayonnaise (recipe follows)

Bring a large pot half full of water to boil. Carefully place the lobsters in the boiling water and cover with a tight-fitting lid. Cook the lobsters for 12 minutes. Remove the lobsters from the pot and plunge into ice water for 3 minutes to stop the cooking process.

Drain the lobsters and remove the claws. Twist

"Barbecued" Spring Lamb with Rosemary

Victor cooks this lamb on a barbecue, adding mesquite or hickory chips to the charcoal and tossing fresh rosemary sprigs onto the white-hot coals.

SERVES 6

3 racks (about 3 pounds) of spring lamb, trimmed of excess fat (6 chops per rack)
1 cup Barbecue Sauce (recipe follows)

Place the lamb racks in a large, shallow baking pan and brush generously with barbecue sauce. Wrap with plastic and refrigerate for 1 hour.
    Preheat the oven to 375°F.
    Roast the lamb, meaty side down, for 20 to 25 minutes, or until the internal temperature registers 130 to 135°F. on an instant-read thermometer. Remove the lamb and set aside to rest for 5 minutes. Slice the racks into individual chops and arrange on a platter.
    Pass the additional sauce separately.

BARBECUE SAUCE

Victor's secret barbecue sauce adds an intense flavor to any marinated meat dish. It can be made two weeks ahead and stored in an airtight container in the refrigerator.

MAKES 3 CUPS

1 cup vegetable oil
½ cup cider vinegar
½ cup water
4 lemons, thinly sliced and seeds removed
½ cup (1 stick) unsalted butter
3 onions, chopped
4 cloves, crushed
3 bay leaves
2 dried chili peppers
1 teaspoon sugar
½ cup A-1 steak sauce or Pickapeppa Jamaican Hot Sauce
1 cup Worcestershire sauce
1 tablespoon peeled and grated fresh ginger
2 tablespoons dry sherry
1 teaspoon soy sauce
Salt and freshly ground black pepper to taste

Combine the ingredients in a large saucepan. Place over medium heat and, stirring, bring the mixture to a simmer. Simmer for 30 minutes, stirring occasionally, until the lemons are soft and the sauce thickens. Discard the lemons and bay leaves and allow the sauce to cool.

Sautéed Bananas

SERVES 6

6 firm, ripe bananas
2 tablespoons sugar
2 tablespoons unsalted butter
2 tablespoons vegetable oil

Slice the bananas and place in a medium mixing bowl. Sprinkle with the sugar and stir gently to combine. In a large sauté pan, melt the butter and oil together over medium heat. When the oil is hot, add the bananas and sauté for 5 minutes, or until lightly browned. Serve immediately.

Stuffed Baked Potatoes

SERVES 6

6 medium Idaho potatoes
½ cup chopped scallions (white and green parts)
¼ cup chopped fresh chives
¼ cup (½ stick) salted butter
2 tablespoons chopped fresh flat-leaf parsley
6 tablespoons grated fresh Parmesan cheese
1 cup heavy cream, heated
Salt and freshly ground black pepper to taste

Preheat the oven to 375°F.

Scrub and rinse the potatoes. Place the potatoes on an oven rack and bake for 60 minutes, or until easily pierced with a metal skewer. Remove from the oven. When the potatoes are cool enough to handle, cut the potatoes in half lengthwise. Do not turn off the oven.

Using a teaspoon, scrape the flesh of the potatoes into a medium mixing bowl, reserving the skins. Combine the scallions, chives, butter, parsley, and 3 tablespoons of the Parmesan cheese with the potatoes and mash until combined. Add the cream to the potato mixture and continue to mash until creamy. Season with salt and pepper.

Spoon the mixture back into the potato skins and sprinkle with the remaining Parmesan cheese. Place the stuffed potatoes on a baking sheet and return to the oven for 10 minutes. Serve hot.

Fresh English Garden Peas

SERVES 6

3 cups shelled peas
¼ cup fresh mint leaves
⅛ teaspoon sugar
¼ teaspoon salt
2 tablespoons salted butter
1 small head Boston lettuce, torn into bite-sized pieces

Bring 2 cups of water to a boil in a medium saucepan over high heat. Add the peas, mint, sugar, and salt and cook for 3 minutes, or until the peas are tender; do not overcook. Strain the peas and place them in a medium mixing bowl. Add the butter and the torn lettuce leaves and toss gently until the butter has melted and the lettuce wilted.

Transfer to a serving dish and serve.

Apple Sorbet with Calvados and Ginger

SERVES 6

5 Golden Delicious apples, peeled, cored, and cut into 1-inch cubes
2 cups sugar
2 teaspoons peeled and grated fresh ginger
Juice of ½ lemon
¼ cup Calvados (apple brandy)

In a heavy medium saucepan, combine the apples with 4 cups of water and the sugar, ginger, and lemon juice. Place over medium heat, bring to a simmer, and simmer for 20 minutes, or until the apples are soft. Transfer the mixture to a food processor and pulse until puréed. Add the Calvados and pulse to blend. Transfer to a bowl, cover, and refrigerate until completely chilled.

Spoon the apple purée into the container of an ice-cream maker and freeze according to the manufacturer's instructions.

Fresh Raspberry Purée

MAKES ¾ CUP

1 pint raspberries, washed and picked over
½ teaspoon sugar
2 tablespoons fresh lemon juice

Combine all the ingredients in a blender or food processor and purée. Pass the purée through a fine sieve, reserving the sauce in a small bowl and discarding the seeds. Serve on the side with any flavor of fruit sorbet.

A Perfect Fall Lunch

WITH ANNE BASS

It takes a brave hostess to allow her first party in her new house to be photographed. Particularly if you're a perfectionist. Anne's taste is so sure, and her organizational qualities so brilliant, that the perfectionist in her had made the house ready for entertaining before she had unpacked a single suitcase

The house is actually a series of barns that were designed and decorated by Peter Marino. Set on vast acreage in southwestern Connecticut, the house is like a compound with some of the barns linked together and some freestanding. Anne likes clean, spare, uncluttered interiors and the rooms are fitted with contemporary upholstered pieces in beige. The minimalist quality extends to the great stone walls, because Anne, who has a breathtaking collection of modern and Impressionist paintings in her New York apartment and her house in Fort Worth, has chosen to put nothing on the walls. It's a notion that I find refreshing in a country setting.

Mrs. Anne Hendricks Bass

CREAMY BUTTERNUT SQUASH SOUP
WITH CAYENNE SEEDS

LEMON PEPPER BISCUITS

SEARED PORK LOIN
WITH HERB LIME BUTTER

JACK DANIEL'S YAM PURÉE
WITH BUTTERED PECANS

SAUTÉED SAVOY
CABBAGE WITH GINGER

MÂCHE, POMEGRANATE,
AND WALNUT SALAD

APPLE FALL WITH MAPLE CREAM

MENU AND RECIPES BY KAREN BURMAN, CHEF

We arrived for lunch on a brisk fall weekend and the menu could not have been better suited to the time and place. The view from the dining room was ablaze with shades of gold and crimson that meshed beautifully with butternut squash soup served in carved-out pumpkins. For a main course, Anne served roast pork loin, which is a big favorite of mine. Pork is something you don't see often enough. It's a particularly good selection around Thanksgiving and Christmas, when everyone feels they'll scream if they see another turkey or capon.

Anne told me she often serves pork in the country and considers it a wonderful alternative to red meat, which she doesn't like. She also likes to use vegetables that are seasonal and grown locally.

As the holidays approach I always think of nuts, apples, and what I call earthy vegetables—yams, turnips, cabbage. I guess Anne does, too. To accompany the roast pork she chose organic yams with buttered pecans and cabbage with ginger, which was out of this world. Our grand finale was a fresh apple tart with maple-flavored whipped cream.

When she entertains in New York City, Anne prefers small seated dinners. She likes them informal but admits it's wonderful to see her guests dressed up when she's gone to a great deal of effort herself. When she gives a dinner she enjoys mixing people who don't know one another. "I consider the party a

success," she told me, "if the guests go on to become friends." In town, her food ranges from Asian to French to Italian. She loves to cook herself, though with her busy life she rarely has the time. Still, she's always reading recipes and most of what is served at home is culled from what she's found.

It's a miracle Anne has time or energy to give dinners at all. A philanthropist and patron of the arts, Anne is an active member of boards and committees too numerous to mention. In New York City alone, she's a board member of the New York City Ballet and the Morgan Library and a council member of three art museums. Her support of ballet and art extends beyond New York City to Fort Worth, Washington, D.C., Paris, and London. When she's not participating in these activities, she spends a lot of time at her own barre practicing her pliés.

Her plate may be more than full, but when she entertains not even the smallest of details gets past her discerning eye. One thing she's extremely particular about is color. She likes everything from china to flowers to correspond to the dinner. Anne prefers small portions and her favorite part of menu planning is selecting the soups, salads, and desserts. Homemade ice cream appears often at her table because, she discovered, it's what her guests like the best. With Anne's eye for detail and sensitivity to color I always know that a dinner at her house will be more than just delicious, it will also be a feast for the eyes.

Creamy Butternut Squash Soup with Cayenne Seeds

Served in sugar dumplings, small pumpkins that make perfect individual serving bowls, this soup is a welcome and surprising appetizer on a cold fall day. It may be made two days ahead and kept refrigerated.

SERVES 8

½ cup (1 stick) unsalted butter
2 large yellow onions, finely chopped
2 teaspoons peeled and grated fresh ginger
2 carrots, peeled and thinly sliced
1 teaspoon dried ground mace
½ teaspoon finely ground white pepper
3 pounds butternut squash, peeled, seeded, and
    cut into 1-inch chunks
1 large yam, peeled and cut into 1-inch chunks
7 cups chicken broth
8 sugar-dumpling pumpkins
Cayenne pepper to taste
Salt to taste

In a large, heavy saucepan, melt the butter over medium heat. When the butter starts to foam, add the onions, ginger, and carrots. Cook until the onion is translucent, about 6 minutes. Add the mace, white pepper, squash, yam, and chicken broth. Bring the mixture to a boil, then reduce to a simmer, cover, and cook until the vegetables are very soft, about 10 minutes. Working in batches, transfer the soup to a blender or food processor and purée. Return the puréed soup to a large saucepan and add a bit of water if the soup is too thick.

Preheat the oven to 375°F.

Forty-five minutes before serving the soup, cut the top off each pumpkin to make a lid and scoop out the seeds and pulp. Reserve 1 cup of the seeds and discard the remaining seeds and pulp. Rinse the seeds and pat them dry. Place the seeds on a small baking tray and sprinkle with cayenne pepper and salt. Bake for 5 minutes, or until lightly browned. Transfer to a small bowl and set aside.

Place the pumpkins and lids flesh-side down in a baking dish, keeping the pairs together so they match. Add ¼ to ½ cup water to the dish and

bake for 15 minutes, or until the flesh starts to yield to gentle pressure. Do not overcook, or they will be too soft to hold the soup.

To serve, reheat the soup if necessary. Ladle the soup into the pumpkin shells, garnish with the spiced seeds, and cover each with a lid.

Lemon Pepper Biscuits

MAKES 16 BISCUITS

3 cups all-purpose flour
1 heaping tablespoon baking powder
1 tablespoon sugar
4½ teaspoons coarsely ground black pepper
1 tablespoon grated lemon zest
¾ teaspoon kosher salt
½ cup (1 stick) unsalted butter, chilled
¾ to 1 cup whole milk
2 tablespoons melted unsalted butter

Preheat the oven to 350°F.

In the container of a food processor, combine the flour, baking powder, sugar, 4 teaspoons of the pepper, the lemon zest, and ½ teaspoon of the salt and pulse to mix. Cut the butter into 8 even pieces and pulse into the flour mixture until it resembles coarse meal. Pour ¾ cup of milk over the mixture and pulse to form a dough; after 8 pulses the dough should form an elastic ball. If it is too dry, add more milk a little at a time until a smooth consistency is achieved.

Turn the dough onto a floured surface and use a rolling pin to roll into a 16 × 4-inch rectangle. Brush the dough with the melted butter and sprinkle the remaining ½ teaspoon of pepper and ¼ teaspoon of salt over the dough. Using a long, sharp knife, cut into 16 even squares.

Separate the squares and place on a baking sheet lined with parchment paper. Bake for 10 minutes, or until golden brown. Remove from the oven. Loosely cover biscuits with a clean kitchen towel and let rest for 5 to 10 minutes before serving.

Seared Pork Loin with Herb Lime Butter

The herb lime butter melted into the sliced pork loin gives it a delicious flavor that balances the sweetness of the yams.

SERVES 4 TO 8

¼ cup fresh lime juice
2 tablespoons grated lime zest
1 teaspoon peeled and minced fresh ginger
3 tablespoons finely chopped fresh cilantro leaves
⅓ cup extra-virgin olive oil
2½ to 3 pounds boneless pork loin
2 tablespoons olive oil
Lime slices, for garnish
Chopped fresh cilantro leaves, for garnish

HERB LIME BUTTER
½ cup (1 stick) unsalted butter, softened
2 teaspoons grated lime zest
1 teaspoon fresh lime juice
2 tablespoons roughly chopped fresh cilantro leaves
1 tablespoon roughly chopped fresh flat-leaf parsley
½ teaspoon kosher salt
¼ teaspoon freshly ground black pepper

In a glass dish that is just large enough to hold the pork, combine the lime juice, lime zest, ginger, cilantro, and olive oil. Trim all the fat from the pork, removing as much of the top layer in one piece as possible (if the fat has already been trimmed, ask your butcher for extra pork fat). Set the fat aside in the refrigerator. Next, use a sharp knife to remove any silver skin (the shiny, silver sheath that coats part of the pork). Place the pork in the marinade, turning to coat, and refrigerate for at least 1 hour, turning once or twice. Meanwhile make the herb lime butter.

Place the softened butter in the container of a food processor and pulse several times until light and fluffy. Add the lime zest, lime juice, cilantro, parsley, salt, and pepper. Process until it begins to turn bright green and the herb leaves are visible. Using a plastic spatula, scrape the butter mixture

(continued on next page)

onto a piece of wax paper and shape into a 1-inch log. Roll tightly in the wax paper and refrigerate.

Remove the pork from the refrigerator and let stand in the marinade at room temperature for 1 hour before cooking.

Preheat the oven to 325°F.

Remove the pork from the marinade and pat dry with paper towels. Tie the pork loin with cooking string every inch to hold its shape. Next, heat 2 tablespoons of oil in a cast-iron pan over high heat, until very hot but not smoking. Sear the pork until brown on all sides. Remove the pan from the heat and place the reserved pork fat on the top side of the pork, covering as much of the pork as possible. Place the pan in the middle of the oven and roast for 45 minutes, or until the pork's internal temperature reads 160°F. when measured with a meat thermometer.

Reduce the oven temperature to 250°F. Remove the pork from the oven, tent loosely in aluminum foil, and let rest for 15 to 20 minutes. Slice the pork thin and arrange on a sheet pan,

overlapping the slices and dotting between with thin slices of the lime butter. Heat the pork in the oven for 5 minutes, just until warmed through. Use a spatula to transfer the pork to a platter garnished with lime slices and cilantro for serving.

Jack Daniel's Yam Purée with Buttered Pecans

Karen suggests using organic yams and pecans, which add an intensity and natural sweetness to this side dish.

SERVES 8

6 pounds organic yams, scrubbed
2 tablespoons Jack Daniel's whiskey (or to taste)
½ cup (1 stick) plus 2 tablespoons unsalted butter
Salt to taste
½ teaspoon white pepper
2 cups organic pecan halves
1 teaspoon kosher salt

Preheat the oven to 400°F.

Prick the yams with a fork and place in a large baking pan that is lined with foil. Bake on the middle shelf for 1 hour, or until they are tender and can easily be pierced with a skewer through the thickest part. Remove from the oven to cool. Reduce the oven temperature to 325°F.

When the yams are cool enough to handle, cut them in half horizontally and scoop the flesh into the bowl of a food processor. Add the whiskey, 8 tablespoons of the butter, and the salt and pepper. Purée until completely smooth. Transfer the mixture to a 2-quart gratin dish or shallow ceramic baking dish.

Spread the pecans in a shallow baking dish in one layer and bake for 10 minutes, or until fragrant. Remove from the oven and place in a medium mixing bowl. While still hot, toss the pecans with the remaining 2 tablespoons of butter and the kosher salt.

Arrange the pecans on top of the purée. Bake for 30 minutes, or until the purée is heated through and the pecans are slightly browned.

Sautéed Savoy Cabbage with Ginger

SERVES 8

1 tablespoon unsalted butter
1 tablespoon olive oil
2 tablespoons shallots, minced
3 tablespoons peeled and minced fresh ginger
12 cups shredded savoy cabbage (about 1½ heads)
¼ to ½ cup chicken stock
1 teaspoon kosher salt
½ teaspoon white pepper

Heat the butter and olive oil in a very large saucepan over medium heat. When the butter has melted, add the shallots and ginger. Cook for 3 minutes, or until the mixture is fragrant and the shallots are translucent. Add the cabbage and stir to coat, then add the chicken stock and cover with a tight-fitting lid. Increase the heat to high and steam for 4 minutes. Uncover the cabbage, stir in the salt and pepper, and continue to cook until tender but still crunchy. Check the seasoning and serve hot.

Mâche, Pomegranate, and Walnut Salad

The intense color of the pomegranate seeds and delicate flavor of the mâche make this a very elegant and festive salad.

SERVES 8

4 pomegranates
1 tablespoon raw sugar
1 tablespoon red wine vinegar
¼ cup extra-virgin olive oil
2 tablespoons canola oil
Salt and freshly ground black pepper to taste
6 cups mâche (lamb's lettuce), rinsed and gently dried
½ cup toasted walnut halves

Halve 2 of the pomegranate and remove the seeds. Set aside. Juice the remaining 2 pomegranates in a juicer or by removing the seeds to a blender and processing for 2 minutes, then extracting the juice by squeezing the seeds through fine muslin. Combine the juice with the sugar and vinegar in a small saucepan. Bring the
(continued on next page)

mixture to a simmer over medium heat and simmer for 5 minutes, stirring to dissolve the sugar. Cook until reduced by half, about 7 minutes. Remove from the heat and cool to room temperature.

Using a hand blender or whisk, slowly add the olive oil to the pomegranate juice mixture, then add the canola oil, blending to combine. Season with salt and pepper.

In a large bowl, toss the mâche with the pomegranate dressing. To serve, divide the salad among 8 plates and garnish with pomegranate seeds and toasted walnuts.

Apple Fall with Maple Cream

The secret of this delicious warming dessert is using lightly salted butter, not usually called for in pastry recipes. The cake will rise above the pan when cooking and then fall when removed from the oven; wait until it falls completely to get its full flavor and an attractively rustic look.

SERVES 8

½ cup (1 stick) plus 3 tablespoons salted butter, softened
11 tablespoons sugar
3 large Mutsu apples
1½ cups all-purpose flour
2 cups whole milk
3 large eggs
1½ teaspoons vanilla extract
Confectioners' sugar, for dusting

MAPLE CREAM
¼ cup maple sugar
1 pint heavy cream

Preheat the oven to 375°F.

Grease a 9-inch springform pan with 2 tablespoons of the butter and dust with 2 tablespoons of the sugar. Peel and core 2 apples and slice very thin. Layer the apple slices in a concentric circle until the bottom of the pan is covered. Sprinkle the apple slices with 1 tablespoon of the sugar and dot with 1 tablespoon of the butter. Place the cake pan on a baking sheet and bake for 30 minutes, or until the apples are tender. Remove from the oven and set aside.

Sift the flour together with 6 tablespoons of the sugar into a large mixing bowl. In a mixing cup, whisk together the milk and eggs. Make a well in the center of the dry ingredients and pour in the milk mixture, whisking constantly, until thoroughly combined.

In a small saucepan, melt the remaining ½ cup of butter with the vanilla over low heat. Gradually pour the butter mixture into the batter, whisking constantly to combine.

Peel and core the remaining apple and slice very thin. Pour the batter over the cooked apple slices and arrange the fresh-cut apple slices on top. Sprinkle with the remaining 2 tablespoons of sugar and bake for 1 hour, or until the cake is puffed, golden, and crusty around the edges. Remove from the oven and cool in the pan on a wire rack for 15 to 20 minutes.

While the cake cools, make the maple cream. Using a whisk, slowly add the maple sugar to the cream and beat briskly until soft peaks form.

Invert the cake onto a serving plate, dust with confectioners' sugar, and serve warm with the maple cream.

Informal

DINNERS

Politically Correct Fare

with Deeda Blair

I never realized how many perfectionists I knew until I embarked on this book project. My friend Deeda Blair falls into that category. There is never a hair out of place. Her makeup is perfect, her clothes are perfect, her house is perfect, and she entertains to perfection. No one would ever expect Deeda to be a dynamo in the field of medical research as well. She's a board member and benefactor of numerous medical institutes and foundations and for the past few years she has devoted her energies to the Harvard AIDS Institute.

The Honorable William McCormick Blair, Jr., and Mrs. Blair

LYCHEE SALAD

LACQUERED DUCK WITH CUMBERLAND SAUCE

WILD RICE WITH GRAPES

ORANGE SALAD

CRISPY OATMEAL COOKIES

COOK: ELSA

As the wife of William McCormick Blair, a former ambassador to Denmark and the Philippines, Deeda is an experienced hostess. She has a talent for making her guests very comfortable in her house whether she knows them or not. Lucky for me and for many others, those years of nonstop embassy entertaining never diminished Deeda's fondness for it.

The Blairs' house was decorated with the help of Billy Baldwin more than thirty years ago and it's as fresh and up-to-date as ever. Deeda succeeded in adapting the grandeur of the eighteenth century to suit the comforts of today, combining eighteenth-century French furniture with modern upholstered pieces.

It's a house made for entertaining. The creaminess of the walls, rugs, and furniture is marvelously flattering and forms the perfect backdrop for guests. The light and luminous quality seems to make everyone look better. Deeda's dining room doesn't really look like a dining room. Instead of a mahogany table with sideboards and extra chairs placed against a wall, she has a large round table that's always covered to the floor and surrounded by cushioned French chairs. At lunchtime the sunlight shimmers through silk curtains made by her dressmaker. At night, she has firelight, candles, and lights that shine subtly through her potted lemon trees. The serene atmosphere coincides with Deeda's preference for small parties. She

rarely has more than eight. "I'd rather talk to people one at a time," she explains, "as I really dislike competitive conversation."

As for her food, what can one say, except that it's as refined as her house—so special that every hostess in Washington uses recipes they begged from Deeda after having been there for lunch or dinner. "I like food that has an unexpected quality to it," she says. "One of my favorite desserts, for example, is a spiral ice cream that goes up like a volcano. We hollow out the center and put powdered chocolate inside, so when you cut it, it pours forth."

The genius of Deeda's graceful way of entertaining is that her dinners and lunches always look like they're the simplest parties to organize. In fact, there's nothing casual about them. Every detail is carefully orchestrated to make the party flow as rhythmically as a Mozart concerto.

Deeda loves couture and that is a fitting analogy for her house and the way she lives and entertains. The furniture, the objects, the flowers, the food are as exquisitely assembled as a custom-made dress— and as lovely to observe as Deeda, who is the jewel in the setting.

Lacquered Duck with Cumberland Sauce

Submerging the ducks in boiling water and hanging them overnight helps to eliminate most of the fat from under the skin and allows the skin to dry. The result is moist meat and crisp skin.

SERVES 6

3 ducks (about 4 pounds each)
3 cups dark corn syrup
3 tablespoons dry sherry
Cumberland Sauce (recipe follows)
6 scallions (white and green parts), thinly sliced
    lengthwise, for garnish
1 bunch of watercress leaves, for garnish

Using the tines of a fork, thoroughly prick the ducks all over, being careful not to prick the meat beneath. Place each duck separately in a pot of boiling water for 5 minutes. Remove the duck from the water, drain thoroughly, and pat dry with paper towels.

Brush the ducks generously with corn syrup and truss with string or butcher's twine. Arrange the ducks side by side in a roasting pan with a rack and refrigerate, uncovered, overnight.

Preheat the oven to 200°F.

Brush the ducks again with the corn syrup. Place 1 tablespoon of sherry in the cavity of each duck. Roast for 2 hours. Increase the oven temperature to 325°F. and roast for 1 hour longer. While the ducks are roasting, baste them frequently, removing any grease with a turkey baster as it accumulates, to prevent flare-ups.

About 30 minutes before serving time, make the Cumberland sauce. Set aside.

When the ducks are tender and deep brown, remove them from the oven, leaving the oven on. Carve the breasts and leg quarters from each duck. Remove the skin and any extra fat; keep the duck pieces warm. Scrape the skin of fat and place the skin on a foil-covered baking sheet. Return to the oven for 10 minutes to crisp.

Meanwhile, cover a serving plate with the sliced scallions and the watercress. Reassemble the meat and the crisped skin and place on the serving plate. Serve with the Cumberland sauce.

CUMBERLAND SAUCE

MAKES 1¼ CUP

1 tablespoon arrowroot powder or 1 teaspoon
    cornstarch
½ cup fresh orange juice
1 cup red currant jelly
½ cup finely julienned orange zest
½ teaspoon dry mustard powder
1 tablespoon dry sherry

Dissolve the arrowroot in the orange juice. Place the red currant jelly in a medium, heavy saucepan and heat over medium heat until the jelly is melted. Add the orange juice mixture, stirring constantly until the mixture is combined. Add the orange zest and the mustard and bring to a boil. Cook over medium heat for 3 minutes, stirring constantly, until the mixture thickens and is clear. Stir in the dry sherry. Keep the sauce warm until ready to serve.

Wild Rice with Grapes

SERVES 6

6 tablespoons (¾ stick) salted butter
1½ cups wild rice
2 cups seedless green grapes, halved
½ cup slivered almonds
Salt and freshly ground black pepper

In a large, heavy saucepan, melt 3 tablespoons of the butter over medium heat. Add the wild rice and stir to coat the rice. Pour in 3 cups of water and bring to a boil. As soon as it boils, cover the rice, reduce the heat to low, and simmer for 50 to 60 minutes, or until all of the water has been absorbed. Remove from the heat and transfer to a medium mixing bowl to cool.

In the same saucepan, melt the remaining 3 tablespoons of butter over low heat. Add the grapes and almonds, stir to combine, and heat through.

Add the grapes and almonds to the wild rice and mix thoroughly. Season with salt and pepper, transfer to a serving bowl, and serve.

Her food is as refined
as her house.

Lychee Salad

The fresh lychees are a delicious addition to this dish; however, if they are unavailable, canned will substitute well.

SERVES 6

½ cup well-chilled cream cheese
2 teaspoons celery salt
2 medium, ripe avocados, halved and seeded
2 tablespoons fresh lemon juice
1 cup fresh lychee nuts, peeled and seeds removed
2 navel oranges, peeled, sliced into ⅛-inch-thick rounds, and seeded
2 scallions (white parts only), thinly sliced diagonally
8 cups romaine lettuce, torn into bite-size pieces
¾ cup finely chopped watercress leaves

DRESSING

1 teaspoon paprika
½ teaspoon dry mustard powder
1 teaspoon salt
1 teaspoon Worcestershire sauce
1 teaspoon minced garlic or onion
½ cup red wine vinegar
2 cups salad oil

With the small end of a melon baller, make balls the size of a marble from the cream cheese. Roll the balls in the celery salt and refrigerate.

With the same small melon baller, make 1 cup of balls from the avocados. Toss with the lemon juice and refrigerate.

In a large mixing bowl, toss together the lychees, oranges, scallions, romaine lettuce, and watercress. Set aside.

To make the dressing, in a medium bowl, combine the paprika, dry mustard, salt, Worcestershire sauce, and garlic. Add the vinegar and whisk in the oil until the dressing is thoroughly combined.

Add the avocado balls and ¾ cup of the dressing to the lychee salad and very gently toss. Taste for seasoning and add more dressing if desired. Sprinkle the cream cheese balls on top and serve.

Orange Salad

The Cointreau is not essential, but it enhances the flavor of this dessert considerably.

SERVES 6

6 oranges
¾ cup finely julienned orange zest
1 cup sugar
½ cup water
Juice of 1 lemon
1 tablespoon Cointreau (optional)
½ cup shelled pistachios, soaked in water for 30 minutes (to remove skins)

Using a very sharp knife, peel the zest from enough of the oranges to make the julienne. Remove all of the rind from all of the oranges and, working over a medium bowl to catch any juice, cut between the membranes to release the segments. Set the segments and juice aside.

In a medium saucepan, combine the sugar and water and stir over low heat until the sugar dissolves. Raise the heat to medium high and bring to a boil. Boil for 1 minute, then add the orange zest. Continue to boil for 1 minute longer, then remove from the heat, add the lemon juice, and cool for 15 minutes.

When cool, stir in the Cointreau if using. Pour the syrup over the orange slices and toss gently. Add the pistachios and chill until serving.

Crispy Oatmeal Cookies

The combination of oats and spices makes a delicious counterpoint to the citrus of the orange salad.

MAKES 4½ DOZEN

1¼ cups margarine, softened
1 cup firmly packed brown sugar
¼ cup granulated sugar
2 large eggs
2 teaspoons vanilla extract
1½ cups all-purpose flour
1 teaspoon baking soda
½ teaspoon salt
1 teaspoon ground cinnamon
¼ teaspoon ground nutmeg
3 cups quick-cooking oats
4 teaspoons finely julienned orange zest
1 cup chopped pecans

Preheat the oven to 375°F.

In a large mixing bowl, beat the margarine, brown sugar, and granulated sugar until creamy, about 5 minutes. Add the eggs and the vanilla and beat until well combined. On a sheet of wax paper, combine the flour, baking soda, salt, cinnamon, and nutmeg. Sift the dry ingredients into the butter mixture and stir to combine using a wooden spoon. Stir in the oats, orange zest, and pecans.

Have ready 2 ungreased cookie sheets. Divide the dough into two equal portions. Working with the first portion, turn the dough onto a lightly floured surface and roll out to a ¼-inch-thick disk. With a 3-inch-round cookie cutter, cut out the cookies and place them 1 inch apart on the cookie sheets. Bake for 10 to 12 minutes, or until crisp. Transfer to a wire rack to cool. Repeat with the remaining cookie dough. Roll any scraps together and cut and bake as above.

Home-Cooking

CHEZ ROCHAS

To watch Carole and François Rochas prepare
and cook dinner is like watching Ginger Rogers and
Fred Astaire dance. They are poetry in motion. As it
happens, the "Some Enchanted Evening" story of
how they met took place in a crowded kitchen. It was
a weekend at a friend's country house where everyone

Monsieur and Madame
François Rochas

MUSHROOM TART

CABBAGE BUNDLES
WITH FOIE GRAS

BUTTERED CARAMEL ICE CREAM

FIGS POACHED IN SAUTERNES

was expected to *mettre la main à la pâte*—that is, put one's hands in the dough and participate in cooking the meals. Carole and François teamed up to prepare a dinner together. She dared a sea-urchin soufflé for the first course; he rose to the occasion and followed it with a canapé of partridge. This inspired team-work soon led to marriage and perpetuation of a gourmet tradition that has delighted their friends for more than twenty years.

In their compact penthouse on the Left Bank, I was, once again, witness to a culinary triumph. Mushroom tart set the stage for an imaginative combination of foie gras wrapped in steamed cabbage; pâté de foie gras is a *spécialité de maison*. Inventiveness didn't stop there, as we delighted in caramel ice cream and figs poached in dessert wine.

For Carole and François, imagining a menu is as exciting as the presentation and delivery. The process starts with going to the market and selecting the best produce according to the seasons and to heartfelt inspiration. What makes their entertaining so unique is that they do everything themselves. The end result is so meticulous and so well organized you would never know how much effort they've put into creating

each event. Undoubtedly, they have their system down to a fine science. As a guest, you barely notice when one of them slips off to the kitchen to give something a stir. The entire meal is prepared during the day. Then, while Carole selects the china and flowers that will best match the menu, François plunges into his cellar book to carefully choose wines that will complement the menu. Often these include wines from Château Lagarosse, their own vineyard in Bordeaux.

I've always believed that you can't be a good cook if you're not a generous person; cooking is made to share. The intensely personal effort they make reflects the joy they derive from sharing their passion for food with others.

After our dinner, I told them that an evening chez Rochas is like dining at a four-star restaurant. They liked the analogy. "Well, Nan," François replied with that tone that indicates they strive not to take themselves too seriously, "we are particularly concerned with maintaining our reputation as fine chefs. Whereas other fashionable restaurants have been deserted, no one has yet deserted our table."

Selecting the best produce according to the seasons and to heartfelt inspiration

THE GRACIOUS SALON.

A PRE-DINNER SNACK FOR THE COOK.

CAROLE OVERSEES THE FLOWERS.

FRESH PRODUCE DICTATES THE MENU.

CAROLE'S CHINA COMPLEMENTS EACH COURSE.

Mushroom Tart

Cèpes, also known as porcini, have a smooth, meaty texture and a wonderful woodsy flavor. They are difficult to obtain fresh but may be found in specialty markets in late spring or autumn. Dried porcini must be softened in hot water for 20 minutes before using.

SERVES 8 TO 10

1 sheet of frozen puff pastry, from a 17¼-ounce package, thawed
¼ cup (4 tablespoons) chopped walnuts
½ cup heavy cream
1 tablespoon salted butter
2 ounces ham in one piece, diced
¼ cup bread crumbs
1 large egg
2¼ pounds (15 cups sliced) cèpe mushrooms, caps removed and finely sliced and stems chopped and reserved
4 tablespoons Parsley-Garlic Butter (recipe follows)

Preheat the oven to 350°F.

On a lightly floured surface, roll out the puff pastry to a 16-inch circle, ¼-inch thick. Gently lay the pastry over a 14-inch tart pan and trim the edges to fit.

In the bowl of a food processor, combine the nuts, cream, butter, ham, bread crumbs, egg, and the chopped mushroom stems. Process until well blended. Spoon the mixture on top of the prepared puff pastry. Arrange the sliced mushroom caps artfully on top of the mushroom stem mixture. Place dollops of the parsley–garlic butter evenly over the surface of the tart. Bake for 35 minutes, or until the pastry is golden and the center is firm.

PARSLEY-GARLIC BUTTER
MAKES 4 TABLESPOONS

4 tablespoons (½ stick) salted butter, softened
2 garlic cloves, minced
2 tablespoons minced fresh flat-leaf parsley

In a small bowl, mix the butter, garlic, and parsley together until well combined. Refrigerate until needed.

Cabbage Bundles with Foie Gras

This dish is elegant in its simplicity, garnished with fleur de sel (the finest of condiment salts) and poivre de tropique (freshly ground pepper), which completes the delicate and full flavors of the foie gras.

SERVES 8

2 large savoy cabbages, washed and separated into whole leaves
2 medium fois gras (uncooked), each sliced into eight ¾-inch-thick slices
Sea salt
Freshly ground black pepper

Bring a large pot of water to a boil. Choose 16 of the largest cabbage leaves and blanch in the boiling water for 5 to 7 minutes, or until the cabbage is tender. Remove the cabbage leaves from the boiling water and allow to cool on paper towels.

Twenty minutes before the foie gras is to be served, prepare 2 steamers in saucepans large enough to hold 8 of the foie gras papillotes. Fill each saucepan with 2 inches of water and bring to a boil.

In the center of each cool cabbage leaf, place a slice of the foie gras and roll the leaf to envelope the foie gras. Once 16 pieces of foie gras are wrapped, prepare 16 pieces of aluminum foil and wrap each cabbage roll in the foil, sealing the edges of the foil tightly.

Place 8 of the papillotes in each steamer and cook for 8 to 10 minutes. Remove from the foil and place two of the rolls on each dinner plate. Sprinkle with salt and pepper to taste.

Buttered Caramel Ice Cream

The intense flavor of this ice cream is attributed to the first and essential step of preparing a rich, dark caramel, well worth the effort.

SERVES 8 TO 10

5 cups milk
1½ cups sugar
14 tablespoons (1¾ sticks) salted butter
10 egg yolks

In a heavy saucepan, scald 1 cup of the milk and keep it warm. In another large, heavy saucepan, combine the sugar and ½ cup water over medium heat. Stir until the sugar dissolves and the liquid is clear. Increase the heat to high and bring the mixture to a boil. Allow the mixture to boil rapidly, without stirring, until it turns to a dark, rich amber color, about 5 minutes. Immediately remove from the heat and slowly add the scalded milk, using caution to prevent splatters. Add the butter and stir to combine until the mixture is smooth. Set aside to cool.

In a separate large saucepan, bring the remaining 4 cups of milk to a boil. In a medium bowl, whisk together the egg yolks. Add 2 tablespoons of the prepared caramel mixture to the egg yolks and then whisk the egg mixture back into the remaining prepared caramel. Slowly add the boiling milk to the caramel mixture, stirring to combine. Cover and refrigerate the mixture until cold, about 45 minutes. Spoon into the container of an ice-cream maker and freeze according to the manufacturer's instructions.

Figs Poached in Sauternes

An early symbol of peace and prosperity, figs are the perfect end to any meal. They may be made up to 2 days ahead and kept covered in the refrigerator.

SERVES 8

16 fresh ripe green figs
4 cups Sauternes

Wash the figs and place them in a single layer in a large saucepan. Pour over enough Sauternes to cover the figs. Place over medium heat and slowly bring to a boil. Reduce the heat and simmer for 12 minutes, or until the figs are soft but not falling apart. Carefully remove the figs and set aside. Increase the heat and bring the Sauternes liquid to a boil. Boil rapidly for 5 minutes, until the liquid has reduced and turned to a light syrup. Allow to cool to room temperature.

To serve, place two figs on each dessert plate and spoon the syrup over. Serve with a scoop of caramel ice cream.

Tuscan Flavors
with the Hambros

Robin Hambro has a magic touch for creating houses as well as a passion for decorating them. During the twenty-five years that my American friend has lived in London, she's moved at least half a dozen times, renovating and decorating the houses herself; and each one is more beautiful than the last. Currently, Robin and her husband, Rupert, who's English, live in Belgravia and spend most weekends at their house in the English countryside.

Two years ago, Rupert went to Tuscany for a weekend and returned to London having bought a dilapidated farmhouse. After the initial shock, Robin once again threw herself into decorating. Perched high enough to offer a panoramic view of the surrounding Tuscan hills, the house now looks exactly as you would want an Italian farmhouse to look. Against whitewashed walls, Robin has arranged furniture with clean, simple lines.

Mr. and Mrs. Rupert Hambro

FRIED SAGE LEAVES
WITH ANCHOVIES

ITALIAN ROASTED CHICKEN

BRUSCHETTA WITH
TOMATO AND BASIL

FRESH FIGS WITH
LAVENDER-INFUSED CREAM

COOK: LUCIANA GUARDUCI

The cook, like the house, is perfectly in keeping with the Tuscan setting: a local woman armed with a repertoire of recipes handed down through the generations. The Italians consider Tuscan cooking the standard for buona san cucina—translated, that means "good healthy cooking." Luciana's food is straightforward and unpretentious.

It is, however, far from boring. Fried sage leaves stuffed with anchovy was a delicious combination that would never have occurred to me in a million years. I've often found that the most straightforward dishes are sometimes the hardest to pull off. How difficult can it be to make a brilliant roast chicken? The answer is: very. Achieving that perfect contrast of crispy skin and moist meat has alluded thousands of us. Lucky Luciana. She has the knack; her roast chicken was done to perfection and seasoned with all the classic herbs found in Tuscan cooking: rosemary, sage, basil, and tarragon. The Tuscan emphasis on fresh and genuine ingredients was evident in the dessert of figs—grown on the property—with cream that was infused with lavender. It was a menu that was uncomplicated and yet full of surprises.

Robin is full of surprises, too. She's a versatile lady who wears many hats. She arrived in London to head the office of American Vogue. She later established an entire fund-raising system for the Covent Garden Opera House and even wrote an opera singers' cookbook. Along the way, she designed jewelry. A connoisseur of art and antiques, she's worked for the past few years at Christie's auction house in London. She rides beautifully, gardens in the country with imagination.

When I asked her how she managed to make all her dinners, lunches, and country weekends work, she confessed to being puzzled herself. "I can't think of any reason," she told me, "except that when you invite fun people whom you adore there is always the possibility of something exciting happening." When it comes to food, Robin's one hard and fast rule is that whatever food you're serving, it must be expandable so that extra people are always welcome, particularly children and their friends. Robin can put a stimulating group together and create a superb dinner party at the drop of a hat. She's always inviting new people to dinner, some of whom she might only have met as recently as the previous night. Her invitations are often so spontaneous that Rupert will walk into the room, turn to her, and ask, "Who are all these people?"

When you invite fun people whom you adore there is always the possibility of something exciting happening.

Fried Sage Leaves with Anchovies

These intensely flavored treats can be passed separately with drinks or served with the chicken.

MAKES 12

24 fresh sage leaves, as large as possible
8 anchovy fillets
1 cup vegetable oil
2 egg yolks
½ cup all-purpose flour

Wash the sage leaves and pat dry with paper towels. In a small food processor or with a mortar and pestle, blend the anchovies into a spreadable paste. Cover the undersides of 12 of the sage leaves with the anchovy paste. Top each with a second leaf and press lightly together.

In a heavy, medium saucepan, heat the oil to 350°F. over medium-high heat.

In a small bowl, whisk the egg yolks until light and fluffy. Place the flour in another bowl. Dip the prepared leaves quickly into the egg yolk mixture and then dredge them in the flour. Fry the leaves, 3 to 4 at a time, for 1 to 2 minutes, or until golden and crispy. Drain on paper towels. Serve warm.

Italian Roasted Chicken

The lemon marinade makes the meat tender and juicy.

SERVES 4 TO 6

1 organic free-range chicken (5 to 6 pounds)
½ cup extra-virgin olive oil
Juice of 2 lemons
1 lemon, halved
2 tablespoons kosher salt

Rinse the chicken inside and out and pat dry with paper towels. Place the chicken in a large, shallow baking dish. Mix the olive oil and lemon juice together in a measuring cup and pour over the chicken. Make sure that the entire chicken has been coated in the marinade. Cover with plastic wrap and refrigerate for 3 to 4 hours.

Preheat the oven to 400°F.

Transfer the chicken to a heavy, shallow roasting pan breast side up; discard the marinade. Rub the chicken all over with the lemon halves and sprinkle with kosher salt.

Roast, basting occasionally, for 1½ hours, or until the chicken is crisp and golden and the juices run clear when the thickest part of the thigh is pierced with a metal skewer. Cut the chicken into serving pieces.

Bruschetta with Tomato and Basil

This perennial favorite can be served warm by adding a cup of diced fresh mozzarella to the tomato mixture and heating the bruschettas in the oven until the cheese melts.

SERVES 4

6 ripe tomatoes
2 garlic cloves
1 tablespoon balsamic vinegar
Salt and freshly ground black pepper to taste
8 1-inch-thick slices Italian peasant bread or
  ciabatta, grilled
2 tablespoons fresh basil leaves, cut into
  chiffonade

Preheat the grill or broiler.

Quarter the tomatoes and place in the bowl of a food processor with the garlic and vinegar. Pulse to combine just until roughly chopped. Season with salt and pepper.

Spoon the tomato mixture onto the grilled bread slices, top with the basil, and serve.

Fresh Figs with Lavender-Infused Cream

Inspired by the abundant quantities of ripe figs on the trees at the Hambros' Tuscan home, this dessert is a heavenly treat.

SERVES 4

½ cup heavy cream
1 sprig of fresh lavender
20 ripe figs
1 tablespoon fresh edible lavender
  or rosemary flowers

Combine the cream and lavender sprig in a small saucepan and slowly bring to a boil over low heat. As soon as it boils, remove it from the heat and set aside to cool. Discard the lavender.

Pour the cream into a small mixing bowl and whisk for 2 to 3 minutes, until very soft peaks are just starting to form. Cover with plastic wrap and refrigerate until ready to serve.

Wash the figs and halve them, setting aside 8 halves for garnish. Working with a small spoon over a bowl, remove the pulp from the remaining fig halves and discard the skins. Divide the fig pulp among 4 dessert plates, top each with 2 of the reserved fig halves, and pour over 2 tablespoons of the lavender cream. Garnish with fresh lavender or rosemary flowers.

Lofty Aspirations

FROM ROSS BLECKNER

Ross Bleckner is as exciting as his paintings, full of energy and vivacity, and he lives exactly the way you would imagine a successful, high-profile artist to live. He owns a five-story loft building in Tribeca, which he renovated years ago. The two top floors—loft-like in design—are his private domain. The décor of the living room/dining room is minimal, but not modern. Rather it's an eclectic mixture of furniture culled from downtown flea markets, a smattering of contemporary pieces, and a touch of the ethnic: antique saris cover the Italian leather sofas, Indian doors act as screens and panels. Very few of his own paintings are on the wall. Instead, he's an avid collector of works by young painters.

Mr. Ross Bleckner

SALAD WITH ROASTED PEARS
AND FENNEL WITH WALNUT VINAIGRETTE

SEARED SEA BASS WITH BABY BOK
CHOY AND GINGER-SOY SAUCE

LAVENDER-HONEY PANNA COTTA
WITH CHILLED STRAWBERRY-CITRUS SOUP

CHEF: LYNN MCNEELY

•

Ross is a rare breed. He's an artist who is at once gifted and social, a party-goer and an occasional party-giver, and he collects friends the way art lovers collect his paintings. I met him in Russia several years ago when we were part of a small group touring St. Petersburg. Ross was responsible for a large measure of the fun on the trip. We happened to be there for Russian New Year and he was invited to a costume party. Ross persuaded a few of us to go along and join in the fun. And so, in a building that was once the KGB headquarters, we danced and drank into the wee hours with a group of charming young Russian artists.

When Ross entertains, it usually is to celebrate a friend or to host a dinner for a charitable cause. He leaves the menu planning up to his cook. Lynn McNeely, a friend and chef who is the proprietor of the restaurant Fressen, cooked our dinner for ten. Although Ross prefers to delegate the cuisine, he does have definite ideas about food. Lynn used to work for him full-time and knows what he likes, which happens to be what Lynn also likes to cook: healthy food with a Mediterranean flair. He especially likes to incorporate interesting grains into the menus. Dairy products are rarely used except if they're organic, like the cream

used in our dessert. Lynn is also a strong believer in organic products and he orders directly from local farmers who grow them. He selects the menu based on the availability of product. Everything we ate that evening was organically grown.

Dinner with Ross is an evening of laughter and nonstop conversation. In fact, it's so lively, and so much fun, that you would never know he doesn't like to entertain. At least that's what he says. If true, that makes him something of a paradox. I think his curmudgeonly attitude is really a product of his profession. When in New York, he's focused on his painting. I've observed the social habits of enough writers and artists to know that when entrenched in their work, they view almost anything outside of that as an intrusion. Not only are they hesitant to give dinners, they're skittish about committing to someone else's invitation. Trust me, Ross, it's the anticipation of entertaining that you hate. Once you're doing it, you adore it; otherwise your guests wouldn't have such a good time.

olive oil. Season with salt and pepper and bake for 40 minutes, or until tender. Remove from the oven and discard the rosemary. When the pears are cool enough to handle, cut each half into ⅛-inch slices and set aside.

Meanwhile, place the fennel slices on another baking sheet and brush with olive oil. Season with salt and pepper and bake for 20 minutes, or until soft and lightly golden. Remove from the oven and set aside.

Combine the greens with the fennel and pear slices. Pour the walnut vinaigrette over the salad and toss lightly to combine. Divide the salad among 6 individual plates and garnish with the toasted walnuts.

Salad with Roasted Pears and Fennel with Walnut Vinaigrette

On an Indian summer day this salad would be delicious with toasted pumpernickel bread and soft cheese. Infused with the aroma of rosemary, the pears are a welcome complement to this flavorful salad.

SERVES 6

½ cup walnut halves, for garnish
1 head of frisée, washed and torn into pieces
1 bunch of watercress, washed and tough stems removed
3 heads of Belgian endive, washed and separated into leaves
3 medium pears, peeled, cored, and halved
6 fresh sprigs of rosemary
1 tablespoon extra-virgin olive oil
Salt and freshly ground black pepper to taste
1 medium fennel bulb, cored and sliced ⅛ inch thick lengthwise
¾ cup Walnut Vinaigrette (recipe follows)

Spread the walnuts on a baking sheet and toast for 5 minutes under a broiler heated to medium. Cool on a wire rack.

Preheat the oven to 350°F.

In a large mixing bowl, combine the frisée, watercress, and endive.

Spear each pear half with a rosemary sprig and place on a baking sheet. Brush the pears with

WALNUT VINAIGRETTE

MAKES ¾ CUP

¼ cup red wine vinegar
1 shallot, finely minced
¼ cup extra-virgin olive oil
¼ cup walnut oil
Salt and freshly ground black pepper to taste

In a small mixing bowl, combine the red wine vinegar and the shallot. Slowly whisk in the olive oil and walnut oil until well incorporated. Season with salt and pepper.

Seared Sea Bass with Baby Bok Choy and Ginger-Soy Sauce

The sauce adds exquisite flavor variations to this simple dish, which is quick, healthy, and fit for a hot summer evening.

SERVES 6

6 striped sea bass fillets (6 ounces each and 1 inch thick)
Salt and freshly ground black pepper to taste
1 tablespoon unsalted butter
9 cups fresh baby bok choy or spinach
1½ cups Ginger-Soy Sauce (recipe follows)
1 tablespoon black sesame seeds, for garnish

(continued on next page)

...An evening of laughter and nonstop conversation.

Season the sea bass with salt and pepper.

Heat the butter in a large sauté pan over medium heat until the butter begins to sizzle. Add the sea bass, skin side down, increase the heat to medium-high, and cook for 4 minutes. Turn the fish over, add ¼ cup of water to the pan, cover, reduce the heat to low, and cook for 3 minutes, until the flesh flakes when separated by a fork.

Meanwhile, place a metal steamer basket in a large pot filled with a small amount of water. Bring the water to a boil, place the bok choy in the steamer, and cook, covered, for 5 minutes, or until the bok choy has wilted.

Divide the steamed bok choy among 6 dinner plates and arrange the fish on each plate. Drizzle each serving with 3 tablespoons of the ginger-soy sauce and sprinkle with black sesame seeds.

GINGER-SOY SAUCE

This dressing is delicious still warm, the flavors of the scallions and tomatoes giving it a rich palate. It would be delicious served over any greens that will hold a warm dressing, such as chicory or spinach.

MAKES 1½ CUPS

Zest and juice of 2 oranges
Zest and juice of 1½ lemons
1 teaspoon rice wine vinegar
1 teaspoon soy sauce
1 teaspoon sugar
1-inch piece of fresh ginger, peeled and finely
    grated
1 garlic clove, minced
2 tablespoons chopped fresh cilantro leaves
¼ cup sesame oil
¼ cup grapeseed oil or canola oil
¼ cup thinly sliced scallions (white parts only)
1 pint cherry tomatoes, halved

In a medium mixing bowl, combine the orange zest and juice, lemon zest and juice, rice wine vinegar, soy sauce, sugar, ginger, garlic, and cilantro. Slowly whisk the sesame oil into the mixture.

Heat a small frying pan over medium heat until it is hot, about 2 minutes. Add the grapeseed oil and continue to heat until the oil is hot. Carefully place the scallions and tomatoes into the hot oil and cook for 1 minute to flavor the oil. Remove

from the heat and immediately pour the hot oil, scallions, and tomatoes into the soy mixture, whisking constantly to emulsify the sauce.

Lavender-Honey Panna Cotta with Chilled Strawberry-Citrus Soup

The lavender honey is Lynn's secret ingredient that makes this panna cotta a taste sensation. It can be made a day ahead and kept chilled in the refrigerator.

SERVES 8

1 quart heavy cream
1 vanilla bean
⅓ cup plus ½ cup sugar
1 tablespoon lavender honey
2 envelopes powdered unflavored gelatin
6 tangelos or small oranges
1 pint fresh strawberries, hulled and thinly sliced

Place the cream, vanilla bean, the ⅓ cup of sugar, and the honey in a heavy saucepan. Bring to a boil, stirring, over medium heat. As soon as the mixture boils, remove it from the heat and allow it to cool until just warm to the touch.

Sprinkle the gelatin into ½ cup of cold water and let stand until very soft, about 2 minutes. Remove from the water and, using a wooden spoon, stir the gelatin into the custard mixture until completely dissolved. Allow the custard to cool completely before pouring into eight 4-ounce ramekins. Chill until set, about 3 hours.

In a small saucepan, combine the ½ cup of sugar with ½ cup water. Stir over medium-low heat to dissolve the sugar. Increase the heat and bring the mixture to a boil. As soon as it boils, remove from the heat and allow it to cool.

Working over a medium bowl to catch any juice and using a sharp knife, remove all peel from the tangelos. Cut between the membranes to release the segments. Stir the strawberries, citrus segments, and any juice into the sugar syrup. Refrigerate until well chilled.

To serve, unmold each panna cotta into a shallow soup plate. Ladle some of the strawberry-citrus soup around each and serve.

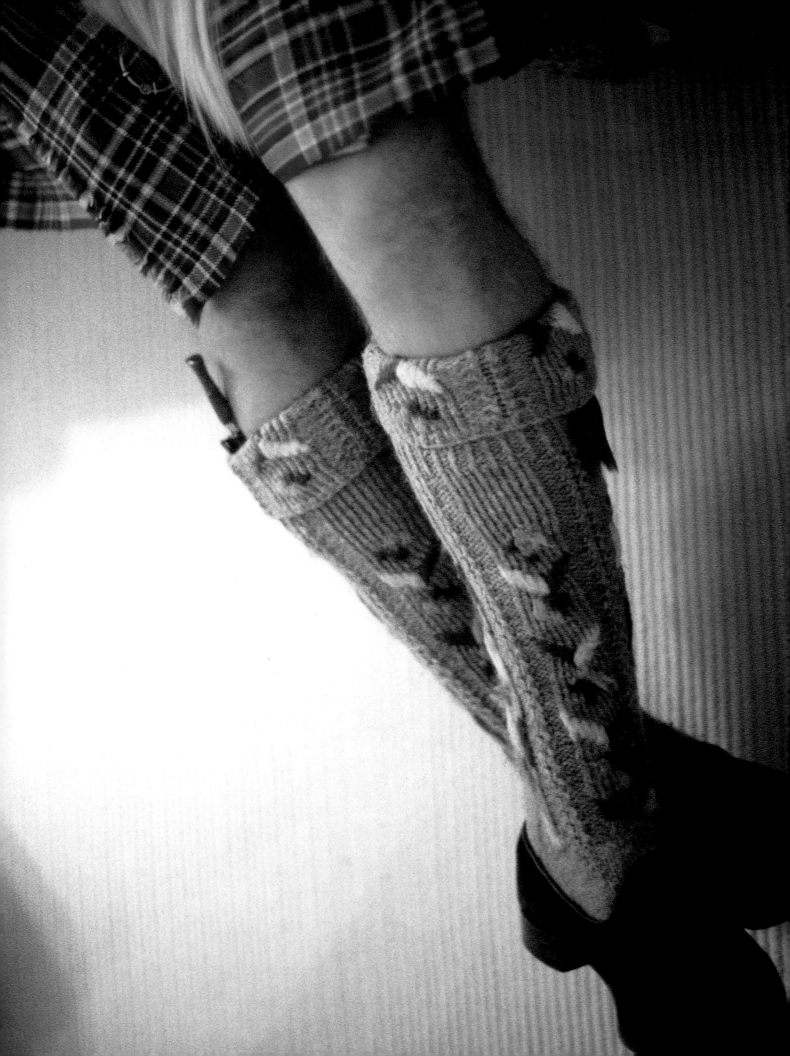

Hacking About
the Highlands

WITH SHEILA DE ROCHAMBEAU

To spend a weekend with Sheila de Rochambeau at Ballachrochan, her centuries-old house in a remote corner of the Scottish Highlands, is a breathtaking, mouthwatering culinary experience. Starting with a breakfast of succulent berries with triple clotted cream and homemade crumpets, the meals that follow get better and better and bigger and bigger.

I must say I've done a lot of adventurous things for great food, but fording a river had never been one of them. That is, not until Sheila offered to entertain

Countess Sheila de Rochambeau

POTATO GALETTES WITH SMOKED SALMON

BRAISED FILLET OF BEEF À LA ROYALE

STEAMED BROCCOLI, PARSNIPS, AND CARROTS

ORANGE FLOATING ISLAND

me in her beloved sixteenth-century Scottish croft situated on the Finhorn River, a bountiful salmon water.

Sheila in her red-nosed Range Rover met me at the Inverness airport. After a lengthy drive that took us past the glorious Cawdor Castle—home of Macbeth—and through countryside right out of a travel brochure, we drove until we reached the edge of the Finhorn. The only way across was for Sheila to floor the gas, plunge into the water, and pray. It was a little hard not to worry; my hostess's accelerator foot had disappeared under water by the time we made it safely to the other side.

Once we made it across the "Rubicon" we enjoyed a four-mile drive past hills covered in purple heather, a sweeping view of the Finhorn Glen, and endless herds of grazing sheep, with no form of human habitation in sight. This magical setting was the perfect balm for our frayed nerves. By the time we reached Sheila's large, rambling house, we were starving.

Watching Sheila prepare a meal is almost as exciting as eating it. She's like a tornado in the kitchen and there's not a pot or pan that doesn't get used. She does it all single-handedly, and chattering away all the while with whomever is in the kitchen. She can whip up four courses without batting an eye. It's almost like watching a magician. If she wanted to, she could be the Julia Child of France, where she lives part of the year. Like Julia Child, she has wit and personality.

The menu for our dinner was chosen so as to require a minimum of cooking during the meal. Our

first course of smoked salmon was layered with a galette of grated potatoes that had been crisply fried in goose fat. She dressed it up with a dollop of crème fraîche and a sprig of dill. She served braised fillet of beef made from the Angus Aberdeen beef for which the Highlands are renowned. Like all foodies I know, she collects recipes with a fury. Our dessert of orange floating island in a sea of Grand Marnier custard was a recipe from Princess Marie-Blanche de Broglie, her dear friend and an admired chef in Paris.

One of the many things that Sheila loves about Ballachrochan is the "adventure" of getting there. Thirty-six friends had to ford the river that night. They treated the evening with a sense of occasion and came dressed accordingly. The men wore their kilts and hand-knitted socks, and the myriad of tartans made for a galaxy of color. Each wore his spencer jacket with a jabot cascading down the front. No jacket was the same in terms of decoration. The adornments were either the wearer's idea or something that may have descended from his grandfather's Highland dress. The women were dressed with delicious femininity.

That dazzling evening was more than Brigadoon come to life. Perhaps the greatest tribute to a hostess is when guests make a supreme effort in anticipation of her own. For my friend Sheila de Rochambeau, entertaining is a reciprocal experience. "I feel strongly," she told me, "that the food and the way I receive my guests is a way of showing the affection I have for so many friends. The chemistry of cooking, beating, and baking is tangible proof."

THE MEN WEAR KILTS TO DINNER.   MY GUEST ROOM.

SILVER AND CRYSTAL, WARMED BY CANDLELIGHT.

MAKING A SPLASH OF AN ENTRANCE. RIGHT: HAGGIS IS A LOCAL SPECIALTY.

Potato Galettes with Smoked Salmon

The warm galettes topped with smoked salmon and dill cream would be delicious for a lunch with a soup as the first course.

SERVES 6

1½ cups grated peeled potato
½ cup goose fat or olive oil
¾ pound smoked salmon
½ cup heavy cream
2 tablespoons finely chopped fresh dill
Julienned zest of 1 lemon

Mold 2 tablespoons of the grated potato into a 2-inch round. Repeat with the remaining potato; you should have about 20 rounds. Place the rounds between paper towels and pat them dry.

In a large frying pan over medium heat, place 1 tablespoon of the fat or oil and heat until it has melted and is quite hot. Fry 5 galettes at a time for 2 to 3 minutes on each side, until they are cooked through and golden brown. Place on a cookie sheet and keep warm in a 200°F. oven. Fry the remaining galettes, adding more fat to the frying pan as needed.

Cut the salmon into squares slightly larger than the galettes and set aside. Pour the cream into a medium mixing bowl and whisk until soft peaks form. Stir in the dill.

To serve, place a warm potato galette on each plate. Top with a piece of smoked salmon, then another galette and another piece of salmon. Garnish with a tablespoon of the dill cream and a piece of lemon zest.

Braised Fillet of Beef
à la Royale

This classic dish from The Grand Masters of
French Cuisine *by Celine Vence and Robert Courtini
is best served with crisp potatoes and colorful steamed
vegetables, like broccoli, parsnips, and carrots. It makes for
a hearty meal on a cold winter night.*

SERVES 6

6 ounces fatback (for larding)
2 sprigs of fresh thyme
½ bay leaf
10 peppercorns, coarsely ground
1 fillet of beef (5 to 5½ pounds)
6 medium onions
2 whole cloves
8 ounces fatback, thinly sliced (for barding)
6 ounces lean veal, thinly sliced
3 sprigs of fresh flat-leaf parsley
1 scallion, white part only
Salt and freshly ground black pepper to taste
2 cups beef broth

Preheat the oven to 275°F.

Cut the rind from the larding fatback, reserving for later use, and cut the fatback into strips about ⅛ inch wide and 2 inches long. Combine 1 sprig of the thyme and the bay leaf in a small bowl and crumble together. Add the peppercorns and roll the strips in the thyme mixture. With a larding needle, insert the strips into the beef.

Cut 5 of the onions into quarters and stick the cloves into the remaining onion.

Place the reserved fatback rind, half of the barding fat, and the veal into a large cast-iron or earthenware pot. Add the onions, parsley, scallion, and the remaining thyme. Place the beef into the pot and cover with the remaining slices of barding fat. Season with salt and pepper and pour the bouillon over. Cover with a tight-fitting lid and cook for six hours, until very tender.

Remove the beef from the pot and place on a hot serving platter. Loosely cover and keep warm until serving. Remove any fat from the surface of the sauce and strain the sauce into a small saucepan. Add 2 tablespoons of cooking liquid and cook over low heat until the sauce has thickened slightly, about 5 minutes. Pour the sauce over the beef and serve.

Orange Floating Island

This recipe was inspired by one in Princess Marie-Blanche de Broglie's Cuisine de Normandie, *which is sadly no longer in print. The meringue can be made ahead and kept for up to 2 days in the refrigerator.*

SERVES 5 TO 6

Zest of 1 orange, removed in strips with a
    vegetable peeler
¼ cup Grand Marnier or other orange liqueur

FOR THE CARAMEL
½ cup sugar
¼ cup water

FOR THE MERINGUE
6 large egg whites, at room temperature
¼ teaspoon cream of tartar
Pinch of salt
¾ cup superfine sugar

FOR THE CRÈME ANGLAISE
1¾ cups milk
4 large egg yolks
⅓ cup sugar

Cut the orange zest into very thin julienne strips. In a small saucepan over medium heat, bring 2 inches of water to a simmer. Add the orange zest and simmer for 10 minutes. Drain and refresh the zest in cold water, then drain on paper towels.

Transfer the zest to a small bowl and pour the Grand Marnier over. Macerate for several hours or overnight. Drain the zest, reserving the Grand Marnier separately.

Fill a 2-quart soufflé dish or a charlotte mold with hot water and set aside while preparing the caramel.

Combine the sugar and water in a medium, heavy saucepan and stir over low heat to dissolve the sugar. Increase the heat to high and bring the mixture to a boil without stirring. Boil rapidly for 5 to 7 minutes, or until the mixture becomes a deep golden color. Remove immediately from the heat.

Pour the water out of the mold and pour the hot caramel sauce into the warmed mold. Tilt the mold in all directions to coat the sides as evenly as possible. Once the caramel has set, turn the mold upside down on wax paper to cool.

Preheat the oven to 275°F.

To make the meringue, place the egg whites in a large bowl and beat with an electric mixer for 3 minutes, until they become foamy. Add the cream of tartar and salt. Gradually increase the mixer speed to high and beat the egg whites for a further 5 minutes, until soft peaks form. Continue to beat the egg whites while adding the sugar, 1 tablespoon at a time, and beating between each addition. Continue to beat the egg whites for several minutes until stiff, shining peaks have formed.

Fold the drained orange zest into the meringue and then gently spoon the meringue to fill the caramelized mold. Place the mold in a large baking dish and half fill with hot water. Bake in the lower third of the oven for 50 minutes, or until the meringue is puffed and lightly browned. Remove the meringue from the baking dish and cool in the mold. When cool, cover the mold with plastic wrap and refrigerate until ready to serve.

To make the crème anglaise, place the milk in a medium, heavy saucepan. Over medium heat, bring the milk to a boil. Immediately remove the milk from the heat and set aside.

In a medium mixing bowl, combine the egg yolks and sugar and beat until they are light and fluffy, about 5 minutes. Add the scalded milk in a thin, flowing stream, whisking constantly to combine. Return the milk and egg mixture to the saucepan, and over medium to low heat cook the mixture, stirring constantly, until it coats the back of a wooden spoon and has thickened. Remove from the heat and stir in the reserved Grand Marnier.

Strain the crème anglaise over a metal bowl set over ice. Stir it occasionally until it is well chilled. Cover the sauce and refrigerate it until serving or for up to 24 hours.

To serve, place a deep, round serving platter over the mold and invert; let the mold stand for a minute or two, then lift off the mold. Pour some of the crème anglaise around the meringue. Serve the remaining sauce separately.

Busy Lives

Lively Meals

Sun-Soaked Days

with the de la Rentas

I've always considered style something that can't really be defined. You just know it when you see it. And for me, Annette and Oscar de la Renta exemplify that mysterious word. The way they talk, the way they stand, the way they live, the way they entertain, and the way they do their houses—style just oozes from their fingertips. If either one rearranges a bunch of flowers, I guarantee you, it will look better. As for their houses, they must have waved a magic wand over them, they've created such fantasies. Whether they're in New York, Connecticut, or the Dominican Republic—Valhalla springs to life.

Two years ago, Annette and Oscar built a private paradise at Punta Cana, located on the southeast coast of Oscar's native country, the Dominican Republic. Instead of rustic, tropical charm, this

Mr. and Mrs. Oscar de la Renta

TOMATO SALAD
WITH CRISP FLAT BREAD

GOLDEN RISOTTO CAKE

CURRIED LOBSTER SALAD

PINEAPPLE TART WITH
TROPICAL FRUIT SALAD

COOK: MARIA SORIANO

beachfront house draws its inspiration from the stone plantation mansions built by grandees in the eighteenth century. The house is a combination of Annette's anglophile tastes, Oscar's enthusiasm for Orientalism, and a Caribbean colonial style. The coral stone walls make for grand living spaces that can withstand the frequent hurricanes—the price of paradise.

At Punta Cana they entertain in the most casual, laid-back way, as is fitting in such a colorful setting. Just as they chose to honor native traditions when they built the house, the food served shows a Creole influence. "What we try to do," says Oscar, "is a hybrid of the local food." With the exception of extra-virgin olive oil, Parmesan cheese, pita bread, and certain condiments, they bring nothing from New York, relying instead on the local fruit, vegetables, and seafood. They enjoy serving things you never see in New York, such as chayote, which is similar to a summer squash except it's grown on a vine. Or bread made from cassava, which is the yucca plant, a mainstay of the Indians who settled there centuries ago.

The guests—usually fourteen strong at every meal—sit like Pavlov's dog drooling as they await the dinner bell. Breakfast is always brought to your room on a tray that's piled high with warm homemade bread, made by Maria, the cook who's been with Oscar for twenty-seven years. Lunch is several different salads and a hot dish or two. We enjoyed a salad of vine-ripened tomatoes and lobster. The de la Rentas rarely serve meat here, preferring instead the fresh, local seafood; the lobster in our salad had been caught

in the wee hours that same morning. Soufflés and pasta are frequently on the menu. Risotto, a house favorite, is cooked a day in advance. The following day, Maria puts it into a pan still cold and then roasts it with mounds of Parmesan cheese.

When it comes to entertaining, you couldn't find two more opposite people than Annette and Oscar. As Annette herself says, "Oscar entertains with ease and I entertain with reluctance." Oscar would entertain the world if he could and can never have enough people around him. Annette, on the other hand, likes a quieter existence. If she had her way she would entertain only very close friends, family, and her dogs. The latter, in fact, far outnumber the houseguests.

But where they come together is at the mutual fountain of love they have for the friends who are always in ready supply at Punta Cana, and they share a talent for making each guest feel special. Because Annette and Oscar never go out when they're at Punta Cana, they import friends from all over the world to stay with them. And what a group they have! I've never met anyone at their house who's not amusing or intellectually stimulating. The conversation is so fast-flying that a meal at Punta Cana is what I imagine dining at the Algonquin Round Table might have been like.

When I asked Oscar how he and Annette consistently congregate people who are equal in humor and intelligence, his answer was very simple: "Nan, we don't have stupid friends."

They **import friends** from **all** over the **world** to stay with them.

Tomato Salad

This salad can be served on its own with crisp flat bread or as part of a buffet lunch.

SERVES 10

8 large vine-ripe tomatoes, peeled if desired
1 tablespoon sugar
1 tablespoon balsamic vinegar
2 tablespoons white wine vinegar
½ cup extra-virgin olive oil
1 teaspoon paprika
Salt and freshly ground black pepper to taste
1 cup fresh basil chiffonade (cut into fine ribbons)

Slice the tomatoes into ¼-inch-thick slices, arrange in a single layer on a platter, and sprinkle with the sugar.

In a medium bowl, combine the vinegars, olive oil, paprika, salt, pepper, and half of the basil. Whisk to combine, then pour over the tomatoes. Marinate for 1 hour before transferring the tomatoes to a large serving bowl and garnishing with the remaining basil to serve.

Golden Risotto Cake

This is a great way use leftover risotto.

SERVES 10

½ cup (1 stick) salted butter
1 onion, diced
3 cups long-grain white rice
1 cup dry white wine
1 tablespoon saffron
5 cups chicken broth, heated
1 tablespoon olive oil
¾ cup freshly grated Parmesan cheese

Melt the butter in a large saucepan over medium heat. Add the onion and cook, stirring, until translucent, about 5 minutes. Add the rice and stir with a wooden spoon to coat the rice well with the butter. Turn the heat to medium-high, add the wine and saffron, and stir continuously in one direction for 3 minutes. As soon as the wine is absorbed, add ½ cup of broth and stir until absorbed. Continue this process, adding the broth ½ cup at a time, until all the broth is absorbed and the rice is creamy and tender, about 50 minutes in all. Remove from the heat and allow to cool.

Heat the olive oil in a large nonstick skillet over medium heat. Spoon the risotto into the pan and flatten into a large cake using the back of a spoon. Cook for 15 minutes, then flip the cake using a large spatula and cook for a further 15 minutes, until golden brown.

To serve, transfer to a large platter and cut into wedges. Pass the Parmesan on the side.

Curried Lobster Salad

*As a variation for this salad, chicken can
be substituted for the lobster.*

SERVES 10

10 cooked lobster tails
1 cup mayonnaise
¼ cup fresh lemon juice
3 tablespoons extra-virgin olive oil
½ tablespoon soy sauce
1½ tablespoons curry powder
Salt and freshly ground black pepper
1 cup finely chopped celery
½ cup finely chopped scallions (white and green
    parts)
3 tablespoons finely chopped fresh flat-leaf
    parsley, for garnish

Remove any red skin from the lobster tails and
cut the meat into chunks.

In a large mixing bowl, combine the mayonnaise, lemon juice, olive oil, soy sauce, and curry
powder and mix well. Season with salt and pepper.
Add the lobster, celery, and scallions to the mixture and use a large spoon to combine.

To serve, mound the salad on a large lettuce-
lined platter and sprinkle with parsley.

Pineapple Tart

*Serve this tropical tart with a fresh fruit salad of mango,
papaya, and kiwi fruit.*

SERVES 10

Pâte Brisée (use half of recipe on page 16)
2 pineapples, trimmed and cut into ½-inch dice
1 cup sugar
1 cinnamon stick
1 teaspoon vanilla extract

Preheat the oven to 400°F.

On a lightly floured surface, roll the pâte
brisée into a 14-inch circle, 1/8 inch thick. Fit the
pastry into an 11-inch tart pan with a removable
bottom. Trim the pastry evenly along the edge of
the pan and chill for 30 minutes.

Line the pastry with parchment paper and
weigh down with dried beans. Bake the pastry
shell for 15 minutes, until light golden brown.
Remove from the oven, discard the beans and
parchment, and allow to cool.

Reduce the oven to 375°F.

In a large saucepan, combine the pineapple,
sugar, cinnamon, and vanilla. Cook over medium-
low heat for 30 minutes, occasionally stirring,
until the fruit breaks down to a compote. Remove
the cinnamon stick. Pour the pineapple mixture
into the pastry shell and bake for 15 minutes.
Cool completely before serving.

THE CLOCK ON THE CHAPEL.

OSCAR AT THE GIN TABLE.

THE OLD-FASHIONED TUB.

ME IN MY OSCAR DE LA "BALMAIN" KAFTAN.

ANNETTE'S FAITHFUL FRIENDS.

Dockside
with Diana Knowles

Every summer of my childhood was spent at Lake Tahoe, in the Sierra Nevada Mountains. To go back and visit with old friends is like revisiting my youth. Nothing has really changed and time has not altered the region's beauty. The lake is as mysterious as ever—its depth is still unknown. The water is just as clear, the air as clean. The terrain is unmanicured and gardens run rampant with wildflowers.

I couldn't imagine writing a book on great hosts without including Diana Knowles. In addition to Lake Tahoe, Diana has houses in San Francisco and Pebble Beach that she shared with her late husband, Gorham Knowles. All of Diana's houses have enormous personality, as does she, but my favorite is Tahoma, her house at Lake Tahoe.

Mrs. Gorham Knowles

FRESH FRUIT JUICE

DOLLAR PANCAKES

FRESH BERRIES WITH
LIME HONEY YOGURT

SCRAMBLED EGGS
WITH ÉCREVISSES

COOK: HAR YEN

Diana's father was Stanley Dollar, the founder of the Dollar Shipping Lines. He fell in love with Lake Tahoe in the 1920s and bought a sizable piece of land. The longtime family tradition of summering at Tahoe continues with Diana, who built her great house on the lake fifteen years ago. It is built into the hills with terraces designed to take advantage of every glorious view. The house overlooks the fathomless emerald lake and Diana's private pier, which flies a huge flag with a dollar sign on it—a witty touch that raised eyebrows until Diana revealed her maiden name.

A visit to Lake Tahoe is, I think, the ultimate California experience—healthy, sporty, and informal. And no one captures the essence of what California entertaining is all about better than Diana. There's also something quintessentially American about her style of entertaining. Her food is the kind of good, old-fashioned American food rarely seen today. Not meat and potatoes, but rather recipes that draw on our varied cultures: chicken tetrazzini, chicken chow mein, meat loaf, and chiles rellenos.

With such a glorious setting and so many delightful ways to spend the day on and around the sparkling water, it's only fitting that Diana loves to start her visitors' days overlooking the lake. Diana's terrace breakfasts are the high point of the day at Tahoma, and whenever I visit her I look forward to the famous Dollar pancakes, a recipe that has remained a family secret until now. All the houseguests—and sometimes neighbors—assemble to discuss what their plans are for the day over a plate of Dollar pancakes, bacon, and eggs scrambled with écrevisses, tiny freshwater crayfish, fresh from the lake. From there everyone goes his or her separate way to enjoy a day of boating, swimming, water skiing, trout fishing, and other outdoorsy pastimes that are on occasion shared with black bears and beavers.

I couldn't imagine writing
a book on great hosts
without including Diana.

Dollar Pancakes

Serve with crispy bacon, link sausage, berries, and a pitcher of warm maple syrup.

SERVES 6

2 large eggs
2 to 3 tablespoons all-purpose flour
2 cups sour cream
½ teaspoon baking soda
½ teaspoon baking powder
½ teaspoon salt
Vegetable oil for the pan

Preheat the oven to 200°F.

Place the eggs in a medium bowl and whisk until light and fluffy. Gradually stir in the flour, mixing well and smoothing out any lumps. Add the sour cream and stir until smooth. Add the baking soda, baking powder, and salt and stir to thoroughly combine.

Heat a medium nonstick frying pan over medium-high heat. Add a small amount of vegetable oil to coat the bottom of the pan. Using a teaspoon, spoon the batter into the pan to make small pancakes. Cook each side for 1 to 2 minutes, until golden brown. Use a spatula to remove the pancakes to a serving plate and place in the oven while making the remaining pancakes.

Fresh Berries with Lime Honey Yogurt

SERVES 6

3 cups plain yogurt
Juice of 2 limes
6 teaspoons honey
6 cups assorted berries, washed and picked over

In a medium bowl, stir together the yogurt and lime juice. Spoon ½ cup of yogurt into the bottom of 6 serving dishes and drizzle each portion with a teaspoon of honey. Add 1 cup of berries to each serving and refrigerate until ready to serve.

Scrambled Eggs with Écrevisses

Caught directly off the pier in Lake Tahoe, écrevisses—the delicately flavored crayfish also known as crawdads—are everyone's favorites when staying at the Knowles home. Four slices of diced smoked salmon or 2 cups of chopped peeled shrimp could be substituted.

SERVES 6 TO 8

30 fresh, live crayfish
12 large eggs
1 cup whole milk
½ cup heavy cream
Salt and freshly ground black pepper
4 tablespoons (½ stick) salted butter

Bring a large pot of salted water to a boil. Add the crayfish, cover tightly, and allow the water to return to a boil. Continue to cook the crayfish for 3 minutes, until they are pink.

Quickly drain the crayfish and immerse in cold water to stop the cooking process. Drain again, remove the tail meat, and set aside.

In a large mixing bowl, combine the eggs, ½ cup of the milk, and ¼ cup of the cream. Whisk until thoroughly combined. Season with salt and pepper.

Melt the butter in a large skillet over medium-low heat. Add the remaining milk and cream to the pan and bring to a simmer. Pour in the whisked egg mixture and stir with a wooden spoon to combine.

Allow the eggs to cook for 2 minutes, and then, using a spatula, gently lift the cooked eggs and tilt the pan to allow the uncooked portion of the eggs to cover the bottom of the pan. Continue this process until the eggs are almost cooked through. Place the crayfish into the pan with the eggs and gently combine to warm the crayfish and finish cooking the eggs.

Divide the eggs among 6 to 8 plates and season with more salt and pepper.

THE MAGIC OF THE VIEW ENSURES A MEMORABLE DAY.

A DELICIOUS MOUTHFUL.

MASSES OF FLOWERS GROW ALONG THE SHORE.

Picnicking
Venetian-style

WITH THE McALPINES

Alistair and Romily McAlpine are among the most lively and fascinating of my friends. Lord McAlpine was the treasurer of the Conservative Party under Margaret Thatcher. Seven years ago, after two of their houses were blown away by the IRA, Alistair and Romily moved to Venice with their daughter Skye, numerous dogs, and collections of stones, glass, sculptures, and all sorts of interesting objects. Their house in Venice, which is actually two houses put together, keeps expanding to accommodate their collections, Alistair's vast library of books, and their visiting friends. Since they moved to Venice, Alistair has become a novelist, but his most recently published book, *Collecting and Display,* focuses on his passion for collecting.

Lord and Lady McAlpine

PLATTER OF CURED AND
SMOKED MEATS: SALAMI,
PROSCIUTTO, SMOKED RABBIT

CRUDITÉS WITH AÏOLI

LITTLE PIZZAS

ROMILY'S POULET ANGLAISE

FLOURLESS CHOCOLATE CAKE

Romily is a true gourmet. For many years, she owned Hobbs, the *ne plus ultra* food shop in London. No one entertains at home with more wit and whimsy than Romily, and relaxation is the key word. One of her favorite ways to bring friends together is to host a picnic lunch on their antique Venetian boat, which was a present to her from Alistair. It was built during the era of comfort and opulence and is the "Rolls-Royce" of canal transportation. All year round—regardless of the weather—Romily loads up the boat with a scrumptious assortment of dishes that she has prepared herself. This moveable feast is digested as the boat glides down the Veneto. What better way to experience the charms of Venice?

The day of our visit, Romily prepared a *déjeuner sur l'herbe* in their courtyard garden. There, on a lazy, sunny autumn afternoon, we feasted on a cold buffet of Italian antipastos that included prosciutto and cheese biscuits, salami, mini pizzas, crudités with aïoli, and smoked rabbit—the latter being the Italian equivalent of a barbecued chicken. (You could substitute smoked duck or turkey breast.)

Fresh ingredients are Romily's priority when she cooks. That's not difficult to achieve with Venice's fabulous food markets. What she prepares for her guests is based on the best of whatever she finds in the

market that particular day. This spontaneous approach finds its way into her style of entertaining. Food isn't at her table only to be consumed; she uses it as part of the decoration. If she's serving bread, a mound of loaves is placed on the table. A cornucopia of fruit and vegetables is piled high and mixed with generous bouquets of flowers. "I like the feeling of abundance at my table," she says.

Abundance at the McAlpines' takes form in more than just food and decoration. In the end, it's what Romily and Alistair bring to the table that makes a lunch or dinner with them so much fun. Both are loaded with such imagination and wit that as a guest you leave their voluptuous seraglio of a house feeling satisfied in both mind and body.

Crudités with Aïoli

The secret to Romily's fabulous aïoli is that she roasts the garlic prior to blending it with the other ingredients and makes it a day in advance. This allows time for all the flavors to marry and makes for an original, robust but mellow dip. The aïoli recipe makes 2 cups.

SERVES 6

AÏOLI
1 head of garlic
1 cup extra-virgin olive oil
2 egg yolks
¼ teaspoon salt
Freshly ground black pepper to taste

2 pounds assorted fresh vegetables (carrots, celery, bell peppers, scallions), rinsed, seeded, and cut into bite-size pieces

Preheat the oven to 400°F.

Slice off enough of the top of the garlic to expose the cloves and brush the exposed cloves with a little of the olive oil. Place the garlic on a small baking sheet and roast for 1 hour, or until browned and fragrant. Remove from the oven and let stand until cool enough to handle.

Place the egg yolks in a large mixing bowl and whisk to combine. Continue whisking while adding the remaining oil in a thin, steady stream. Whisk constantly for 4 minutes, or until the mixture is thick and emulsified.

Remove the roasted garlic cloves from their skins and place in a mortar and pestle. Grind the garlic to a paste. Stir into the egg-yolk mixture and season with salt and pepper. Transfer to a tightly sealed container and refrigerate overnight. To serve, spoon the aïoli into a serving dish and accompany with the vegetables.

Little Pizzas

These delightful little pizzas are Romily's favorites for an easy appertizer. Served "just warm," they make a delicious mouthful.

MAKES SIX 8-INCH PIZZAS

1 package of fresh or thawed frozen pizza dough
¼ cup fine cornmeal
6 tablespoons extra-virgin olive oil
6 plum tomatoes, stemmed, seeded, and diced
1 red onion, very thinly sliced
1 cup chopped black olives, such as Gaeta
½ pound fresh buffalo-milk mozzarella, thinly sliced
½ teaspoon chopped fresh oregano
Salt and freshly ground black pepper to taste

Place a large pizza stone on the middle shelf of the oven. Preheat the oven to 500°F.

Divide the pizza dough into 6 equal portions. Lightly flour a work surface and, using a rolling pin, roll each dough portion into an 8-inch disk. Lightly dust a round pizza peel with cornmeal and transfer the disks onto the peel.

Brush each pizza with 1 tablespoon of the olive oil. Spread the tomatoes over each pizza and top with the onion slices, olives, cheese, and oregano. Sprinkle with salt and pepper.

Use the pizza peel to slide the pizzas onto the pizza stone in the oven. Bake the pizzas for 5 to 7 minutes, or until the crusts are golden and the cheese bubbly. Serve immediately.

It's what Romily and Alistair bring to the table that makes a lunch or dinner with them so much fun.

A VENETIAN SPECIALTY: STRAWBERRY WINE.

A LAZY AFTERNOON OF GOOD FOOD AND CONVERSATION.

EXPLORING THE WONDERS OF VENICE.

ENJOYING A HOMEMADE GELATO AFTER LUNCH.

white pepper and stir until well blended. Chill covered in the refrigerator until ready to serve.

Thinly slice the chicken breasts and arrange on a serving tray. Serve the dressing alongside or drizzled over the chicken.

Flourless Chocolate Cake

This cake is an enduring classic, requiring little preparation time. The delicious result is best served warm with a fruit coulis and a smart Riesling.

MAKES ONE 9-INCH CAKE

15 ounces good-quality semisweet chocolate, chopped
1 cup (2 sticks) unsalted butter
6 large eggs, lightly beaten
Pinch of salt

Preheat the oven to 350°F. Grease and lightly flour a 9-inch cake or springform pan.

Place the chocolate and butter in a double boiler or stainless-steel bowl set over a pot of simmering water. Stir occasionally with a wooden spoon until the mixture has melted and combined, about 5 minutes. Remove from the heat and set aside.

Place the eggs and salt in a metal bowl that will rest on top of a saucepan containing 2 inches of boiling water. Whisk until the mixture is warm to the touch. Remove from the heat and, with an electric mixer, beat the eggs until they have tripled in volume.

Fold the egg mixture into the combined melted chocolate and butter. Mix until thoroughly combined. Pour the mixture into the prepared pan and bake the cake for 25 minutes, or until a toothpick inserted into the center comes out almost clean. Cool completely on a wire rack before turning onto a cake platter to serve.

Romily's Poulet Anglaise

This was one of the most popular dishes at Hobbs, most deserving a reprise as it is the perfect picnic food, portable yet delicious.

SERVES 6 TO 8

4 cups vegetable or chicken stock
6 skinless chicken breast halves
1 cup natural yogurt
1 teaspoon black poppy seeds
1 English cucumber, peeled and finely diced
2 shallots, minced
¼ cup chopped fresh curly-leaf parsley
Finely ground white pepper to taste

Pour the stock into a large saucepan and bring to a boil. Reduce the heat to a simmer, add the chicken breasts, and poach in the stock for 15 minutes, or until cooked through and tender. Remove the chicken from the stock and set aside.

In a large bowl, combine the yogurt, black poppy seeds, cucumber, shallots, parsley, and

Weighing Anchor
with Valentino

"A host is like a general: calamities often reveal his genius." At least that's what the Roman poet Horace said, some time around 65 B.C. Valentino, another great Roman, certainly fits that description. And so what was meant to be a weekend of swimming, water skiing, and underwater exploration on the Capri coast turned into an eating fest when rough seas grounded our activities. We may have been parked at the dock, but we still enjoyed the glamour of Valentino's sleek eighty-foot yacht, the *T. M. Blue One.*

Mr. Valentino Garavani

BARLEY SEAFOOD SALAD

FRESH SEAFOOD RAVIOLI
WITH SEA BASS SAUCE

CAPRESE CAKE

COOK: SAVINO LA ROLLA

From his clothes to his houses to his boat, "impeccable" is the ideal word to describe everything in Valentino's life. He builds his days like an architectural plan and then executes what he imagines to a tee. Entertaining is just one way he exercises his passion for beauty. He has a penchant for linen tablecloths, custom-made for him by Italian artisans, and china, which he collects in abundance. But the real focal point of his dinners is the food. He likes to say that because he's Italian he has a winning ticket when it comes to menus. As far as he's concerned, his native cuisine is the most diverse, delicious, and beloved by all. And visually speaking, it makes for a beautiful presentation.

Valentino has a remarkable sense of flavor and textural combination. His food is imaginative and creative, and he designs menus in much the same way he designs his fashions. For each meal, he prepares a menu book for his chef, sketching out what he wants. He then spends time in the kitchen developing the recipes with the chef, specifying ingredients and discussing how to realize the dish he has in mind—not just how it will taste, but also how the dish will be presented.

There are no fancy meals on the *T. M. Blue One.* Instead, he opts for simplified entertaining. There's always loads of pasta—pesto sauce is a particular favorite—and naturally an emphasis on fish and seafood that's pristinely fresh and delivered directly to the boat by the local fishermen, who offer their daily catch. For our lunch, seafood turned up in the salad and the homemade ravioli was stuffed with fish.

Valentino is a warm, gentle man who thinks more about his guest's comfort than his own. The *T. M. Blue One* carries all the pleasures of home out to sea. Everything has been thought of for the hungry passenger; enormous fruit baskets and bowls of nuts are available at all times for those whose appetites are sharpened by the sea air. The boat has every creature comfort, down to monogrammed bathrobes.

I can't think of anyone I'd rather be stranded with than Valentino. While winds howled outside and the waters churned around us, inside the *T. M. Blue One*'s stabilizers calmed the storm's force to a gentle rocking. We watched videos, chatted about fashion—he even designed a dress for me—and indulged in luxurious naps. Outside the storm rattled on, but in the comfort of Valentino's floating retreat we swayed to the smooth rhythm of engaging conversation and easy, delicious meals.

EVERYTHING MADE TO MEASURE.

VALENTINO CREATES VALENTINO FOR ME, BELOW.

MAKING THE RAVIOLI.   MY STATEROOM.

Valentino

24 cherrystone clams
¼ teaspoon white wine vinegar
3 small squid, cleaned
18 medium shrimp, peeled
2 tomatoes, peeled, seeded, and diced
¼ cup chopped fresh basil
¼ cup chopped fresh flat-leaf parsley
½ cup extra-virgin olive oil
Juice of 2 lemons
Freshly ground black pepper to taste

Bring a large pot of water to a simmer, add the baby octopus, and cook uncovered for 1½ hours. Set aside to cool slightly.

Meanwhile, in a medium saucepan, bring 3 cups of water to a boil. Add the barley, return to a boil, then reduce the heat to low. Cover and simmer for 30 to 40 minutes, or until the water is absorbed and the barley is tender but not soft. Transfer the barley to a large mixing bowl to cool.

In a medium saucepan, bring 3 cups of salted water to a boil. Add the zucchini, carrots, and peas and blanch for 1 minute. Drain and shock in cold water to stop the cooking process. Drain well and add to the mixing bowl with the barley. Add the red and yellow bell peppers to the bowl.

Bring 2 inches of water to a boil in a large saucepan with a steamer insert. Place the clams in the steamer, cover, and steam for 5 minutes, or just until the shells open. Remove the clams from the shells and place in a small bowl.

Bring a large saucepan of water to a boil. Add the vinegar and squid and boil for 3 to 4 minutes. Add the shrimp and boil for 1 to 2 minutes longer. Drain well and set aside.

When the squid and octopus are somewhat cool, chop them and add to the mixing bowl with the barley and vegetables. Add the tomatoes, shrimp, and clams and stir to combine. Place the basil, parsley, olive oil, lemon juice, and pepper in a small bowl and whisk to combine. Pour over the salad and gently toss, then transfer to a platter to serve.

Barley Seafood Salad

This typically elegant dish, inspired by the wonderfully fresh seafood available in the Capri markets, would be perfect served as a light lunch with an avocado salad. The octopus must cook gently for 1½ hours to ensure tenderness; if you are pressed for time, substitute another favorite shellfish or simply leave it out.

SERVES 6

12 baby octopus, cleaned
1½ cups pearl barley
Salt to taste
2 zucchini, diced
2 carrots, peeled and diced
1 cup fresh peas
½ red bell pepper, seeded and diced
½ yellow bell pepper, seeded and diced

Fresh Seafood Ravioli with Sea Bass Sauce

Valentino is known for designing delicious fillings for the homemade ravioli that is so often served when he entertains. In Capri, where fresh seafood is plentiful, this ravioli is not only a favorite with guests but also easy to prepare for a casual lunch on board the T. M. Blue One.

SERVES 6

1 pound sea bass fillets
3 tablespoons extra-virgin olive oil
Salt and freshly ground black pepper to taste
1 medium onion, finely chopped
1 tablespoon finely chopped fresh thyme leaves
½ pound squid, cleaned and chopped
½ pound shrimp, peeled and chopped
1 egg, lightly beaten
1 tablespoon finely chopped fresh flat-leaf parsley
1 pound plus 2 ounces all-purpose flour
   (3½ cups)
4 large eggs
Sea Bass Sauce (recipe follows)

Preheat the oven to 350°F.

Brush the fish with 1 tablespoon of the olive oil, place in a baking dish, and season with salt and pepper. Bake for 20 minutes, or until the fish is cooked through. Remove from the oven and allow to cool.

Heat a medium sauté pan over medium heat and add the remaining 2 tablespoons of olive oil. Add the onion and thyme and sauté for 3 minutes, until the onion is translucent. Add the chopped squid and shrimp and cook, stirring, for 3 minutes. Flake the sea bass with your fingers and stir into the squid mixture. Cook for 4 to 5 minutes, stirring occasionally, and then remove from the heat to cool for 15 minutes.

Add the egg to the seafood mixture and combine well. Stir in the chopped parsley and season with salt and pepper. Transfer to a medium mixing bowl to cool.

Mound the flour on a work surface and make a well in the center. Break the 4 eggs into the well and, using a fork, carefully beat to incorporate the yolks with the whites. Gradually draw in flour from the outside of the well until a dough begins to form. When all the flour is incorporated, knead the dough lightly until it is smooth in texture. Divide the dough into 2 equal portions and, using a floured rolling pin, roll each into a thin rectangular sheet, approximately ⅛ inch thick.

Place tablespoons of filling at 1-inch intervals over 1 entire sheet of pasta. Gently lay the second sheet on top, pressing around the mounds of filling with your fingers. With a serrated rolling cutter or a sharp knife, cut between the filling mounds to create individual raviolis, pressing the edges well to seal.

Bring a large saucepan of salted water to a boil. Add the ravioli and cook for 5 to 7 minutes, or until the pasta is al dente. Drain.

Place 6 ravioli on each plate, top with some of the sea bass sauce, and pass the remaining sauce around the table.

SEA BASS SAUCE

This sauce is rich and flavorful and would be perfect served over any simple pasta such as spaghetti or penne. The addition of a meaty fish fillet gives the sauce a moist and delicious texture.

SERVES 6

½ cup extra-virgin olive oil
½ onion, minced
2 garlic cloves, thinly sliced
1 dried hot red pepper
2 sea bass fillets, cubed (about 1 pound)
2 tablespoons Cognac
7 large ripe tomatoes, peeled, seeded, and cut into
   ½-inch cubes (about 2 pounds)
½ cup pine nuts
½ cup fresh basil leaves, lightly packed

Heat a large sauté pan over medium heat and add the oil. When the oil is hot, add the onion and sauté for 3 minutes, until golden. Add the garlic and the pepper and sauté for 2 minutes, then add the fish cubes and cook, stirring frequently, for an additional 2 minutes, until the fish is just cooked through.

(continued on next page)

He designs menus
in much the same way he
designs his collections.

Preheat the oven to 250°F.

Add the Cognac to the pan and carefully ignite the liquid by just touching it with a lit match. Allow the flame to burn until it extinguishes itself; this will burn off the alcohol. Add the tomatoes and cook for 20 minutes, stirring occasionally, until the tomatoes have become saucelike in consistency. Remove from the heat and set aside.

Meanwhile, in a hot, dry skillet toast the pine nuts for 2 to 3 minutes until just golden brown, being careful not to burn them. Transfer the nuts to a plate immediately to cool.

Transfer the sauce to the bowl of a food processor and pulse five times, just to incorporate the ingredients. Transfer the sauce to a heatproof serving bowl and keep warm in the oven.

When ready to serve, stir in the fresh basil and garnish the sauce with the toasted pine nuts.

Caprese Cake

This flourless chocolate cake, a specialty of Capri and a favorite of Valentino, is delicious served with vanilla ice cream.

SERVES 8

10 tablespoons (1¼ sticks) unsalted butter, plus extra for greasing the pan
Flour for dusing the pan
3½ ounces mini Melba toasts (available at most supermarkets)
2 tablespoons margarine
5 large eggs
¾ cup sugar
1 teaspoon baking powder
Pinch of salt
1 cup ground almonds
1 pound bittersweet chocolate, grated, plus more for garnish
Confectioners' sugar, for garnish

Preheat the oven to 350°F.

Grease a 10-inch round springform pan with extra butter and dust it with flour.

Place the Melba toasts in the bowl of a food processor. Pulse until finely crushed.
In a small saucepan, melt the 10 tablespoons of butter and the margarine over low heat. Set aside.
In a medium mixing bowl, beat the eggs and sugar until light and fluffy. Add the crushed toasts, baking powder, salt, and almonds and stir to combine. Add the chocolate and the melted butter and margarine and mix together until well blended.

Pour the cake mixture into the prepared pan and bake for 50 to 55 minutes; a toothpick inserted in the center should come out almost clean. Cool the cake on a wire rack. Invert onto a serving plate and garnish with a sprinkle of confectioners' sugar and grated chocolate.

After the Hunt

chez d'Ornano

Isabelle and Hubertd' Ornano divide their time between a Paris duplex and La Renaudière, their six-thousand-acre estate in the Loire Valley. When they invited me to their country house for an autumn shooting weekend, I jumped at the chance. So there I was, on a raw, cold Saturday in November, realizing my fantasy.

A boar hunt isn't just for sport; the French government asks estate owners to cull their boar populations once a year to prevent the herds from overrunning and damaging the countryside. The shoot itself lasts for about two hours. The hunters position themselves in the woods and the beaters make noise to flush out the boars, who then charge across an

Count and Countess Hubert d'Ornano

PIZZA "RENAUDIÈRE"

MOUSSAKA

TRUFFLED SCRAMBLED EGGS EN CROÛTE

FRUIT CRUMBLE

COOK: GERARD GAUSSET

open field. Emilio Botin, the d'Ornanos' son-in-law, was my shooting partner, which is to say, while he aimed and fired, I flattened myself against a tree. At one point, I wished I were the tree when one of these large, ferocious animals with huge tusks charged toward us. Fortunately, Emilio is a crack shot and got him right between the eyes before I could be turned into shish kebab. My jangled nerves were soon calmed when we returned to the house for lunch. There we were greeted with bull shots and a hearty buffet that included moussaka, scrambled eggs with truffles encased in a puff pastry, and pizza à la d'Ornano.

Hubert d'Ornano is the CEO and chairman of the board of Sisley, the botanical skincare and cosmetics company that he founded with his wife Isabelle, who serves as the company's director of communications and product development. Just as they work in tandem professionally, they are also a well-matched team in their personal life. Both have a love of art, design, and every other aspect of what Cecil Beaton called "the living arts." For weekends at La Renaudière they create the guest list together. Hubert oversees the shoots and everything connected with the property, while Isabelle takes charge of the house, the guest rooms, the menus, the flowers. Wine is Hubert's domain.

My stay with them was like a step back in time. Age-old customs and traditions are still intact. Classic shooting attire is expected. After breaking for lunch, guests enjoy a second stand in the woods, and at the end of that round of shooting a marvelous tea is served. On Saturday evening there's a *tableau de*

chasse, which is a firelit ceremony to honor the boar that includes everyone involved with the hunt. Hubert gives a great deal of importance to the tradition of respecting the game. He thanks the keeper, the beaters, and all those who helped with the shoot, and then the houseguests who shot that day do the same.

Traditional, however, does not mean formal. Although every detail of the weekend, from creature comforts to the scrumptious food, has been well thought out, Isabelle entertains in the most relaxed manner. She doesn't like to linger at the table, so both lunch and dinner are always served buffet-style, even if it's for six. Accordingly, she doesn't go in for traditional French menus with courses of fish, meat, salad, and cheese. Instead she likes the exotic. She enjoys collecting recipes and has her talented chef, Gerard Gausset, adapt them to her own taste. Her Polish heritage also finds its way into the menus. She likes kasha, but mixes the crunchy grain with something as unlikely as fresh foie gras.

Both Hubert and Isabelle manage to make their houseguests feel as cared for as members of the family. And family is a key element. On weekends—at anytime of year—the d'Ornanos' grown children arrive with their offspring. As a result, a tremendous spirit flows through the house. I left the weekend knowing that through the next generation of d'Ornanos there will be a continuation of a way of life that honors tradition and the world that their parents have created—a seamless blend of splendor, simplicity, and originality.

Pizza "Renaudière"

Made with puff pastry, this pizza melts in the mouth and is a favorite of the d'Ornanos, who served it as part of a buffet lunch. The harissa adds spice to the sauce base and can be adjusted according to taste. It would stand on its own served with salad. Of course you can adapt the topping to your own preferences.

SERVES 10 TO 12

3 tablespoons extra-virgin olive oil

4 large onions, chopped

1 teaspoon harissa (available at Middle Eastern groceries), or Tabasco sauce

1 garlic clove, minced

5 firm, ripe tomatoes

1 small bunch of fresh basil (about 3 cups of leaves)

1 teaspoon sugar

2 sheets of frozen puff pastry, thawed

5 ounces fresh mozzarella cheese, cut into 12 thin slices

8 ounces ham (2 slices), cut into strips

Salt and freshly ground black pepper to taste

1 small bunch of oregano (about 1½ cups leaves), chopped

10 whole anchovies

24 black olives, pitted

6 ounces grated Gruyère cheese (about 2 cups)

In a large saucepan, heat the oil over medium heat. Add the onions and cook, stirring occasionally, until the onions are soft and golden, about 10 minutes. Add the harissa and garlic and cook for 3 minutes longer. Chop 4 of the tomatoes. Add the chopped tomatoes and half of the basil to the pan with the sugar. Cook for 20 minutes, or until any liquid has evaporated and the mixture is thick. Set the mixture aside.

Preheat the oven to 375°F.

On a lightly floured work surface, roll out the pastry into two 12 × 16-inch rectangles and place on 2 large, ungreased baking sheets. Slice the remaining tomato thin. Spread a thin layer of tomato sauce over each of the crusts and top each with half of the mozzarella slices, half of the ham, half of the tomato, and remaining half of the basil leaves. Sprinkle each with salt and pepper, then scatter the oregano leaves, anchovies, and black olives over both pizzas. Place in the oven and bake for 50 minutes, or until the pastry is puffed and golden. Remove and sprinkle each with half of the Gruyère, return to the oven, and cook a further 10 minutes, or until the cheese has melted. Allow to cool slightly before serving in slices.

Moussaka

Adapting recipes like this is one of Gerard's specialties.

SERVES 10

6 large eggplants (about 1½ pounds each)

4 tablespoons kosher salt

1 cup plus 2 teaspoons olive oil

Salt and freshly ground black pepper to taste

¼ teaspoon white pepper

¼ teaspoon ground nutmeg

¼ teaspoon ground ginger

¼ teaspoon ground cinnamon

1 large onion, finely chopped

2 garlic cloves, minced

1 teaspoon harissa (available at Middle Eastern groceries), or Tabasco sauce

2½ pounds lean ground lamb

1 cup chopped fresh flat-leaf parsley

2 cups cooked white rice

6 cups Tomato Sauce (recipe follows)

½ cup grated Gruyère cheese

15 minutes. Stir in the parsley, season with salt and pepper, and set aside.

Grease a 4-quart oval baking dish with olive oil. Lay some of the eggplant slices decoratively in a fanlike pattern around the edges, allowing the slices to reach over the edge of the dish.

Arrange a layer of the eggplant in the bottom of the dish, spread a thin layer of rice over it, and top with half of the lamb mixture. Repeat with more of the eggplant and the remaining rice and lamb, and finish with a layer of eggplant.

Spoon the tomato sauce over the center of the dish and fold the overhanging eggplant slices into the sauce so that they form a decorative mound around the edge. Sprinkle with the Gruyère and bake for 1 hour, or until the top is golden and bubbling.

TOMATO SAUCE
MAKES 6 CUPS

3 tablespoons olive oil
1 large onion, chopped
3½ pounds tomatoes, peeled, seeded, and cut
    into 1-inch pieces
1 teaspoon sugar
½ cup chopped fresh flat-leaf parsley
Salt and freshly ground black pepper to taste

Heat the oil in a medium saucepan over medium heat. Add the onion and cook for 5 minutes, or until the onion is soft and slightly golden. Add the tomatoes and sugar and cook for 20 minutes, until the liquid has evaporated and the mixture thickens. Stir in the parsley and season with salt and pepper.

Slice the eggplants lengthwise into ¼-inch-thick slices. Generously sprinkle each slice with coarse salt and allow them to rest for 1 hour. With a clean kitchen towel or paper towel, dry the slices, removing any excess salt.

Preheat the oven to 375°F.

Heat ¼ cup of the oil in a large frying pan over medium heat. Fry one quarter of the eggplant slices in a single layer, until they are golden on both sides. Sprinkle with a little salt, black pepper, white pepper, nutmeg, ginger, and cinnamon, then remove and place on a plate lined with paper towels. Repeat with the remaining ¾ cup of oil and the eggplant slices.

In the same frying pan, heat the remaining 2 teaspoons of oil over medium heat and add the onion. Cook, stirring, until soft and slightly golden, about 5 minutes. Add the garlic and harissa and cook a further 2 minutes. Add the ground lamb and cook, stirring, until the lamb is cooked through and slightly golden, about

Truffled Scrambled Eggs en Croûte

If fresh truffles are not available, the recipe is equally delicious with 8 ounces of diced prosciutto or smoked salmon.

SERVES 10

2 sheets of frozen puff pastry, thawed for 45
   minutes
1 egg yolk plus 24 large eggs
3 tablespoons port or Cognac
2 fresh truffles
Salt and freshly ground black pepper to taste
½ cup (1 stick) salted butter
½ cup crème fraîche
2 tablespoons finely chopped fresh herbs,
   such as dill, basil, and chives
3 tablespoons finely chopped fresh
   flat-leaf parsley

Preheat the oven to 375°F.

On a lightly floured work surface, roll out the pastry into two 12-inch squares or circles, ¼ inch thick. Place 1 pastry sheet on a heavy baking sheet. Lightly place the second on top of the first and, using a sharp knife, score 1-inch cuts around the edges of the top sheet. Lightly beat the egg yolk and brush the top within the scored marks. Bake for 20 minutes, or until the pastry has puffed to 3 inches. Remove and allow to cool slightly before removing the "lid." Remove and discard any uncooked layers that remain inside the "bowl." Place the pastry bowl on a platter lined with a napkin (to prevent slipping) and set aside while preparing the eggs.

In a small saucepan over low heat, bring the port to a slow simmer. Add the truffles and cook for 3 minutes. Remove the truffles with a slotted spoon, roughly chop, and set aside.

Place the eggs in a very large bowl and beat lightly until combined. Season with salt and pepper. In a very large sauté pan over medium heat, melt the butter, turning the pan to coat all sides. Add the eggs and stir over medium heat until they begin to cook, about 2 minutes. While still stirring, gradually add the crème fraîche. Stir in the truffles and the fresh herbs. Continue to cook for 5 minutes, or until the eggs are cooked and fluffy.

Fill the pastry bowl with the cooked eggs. Replace the lid, slightly askew to give the dish an attractive look, and sprinkle with parsley. Serve immediately.

Fruit Crumble

SERVES 10

4½ pounds Golden Delicious apples,
   peeled and cored
1 tablespoon plus ¼ cup (½ stick) very cold
   unsalted butter
½ cup golden raisins
2 cups packed dark brown sugar
1 teaspoon vanilla extract
1 teaspoon ground cinnamon
1 cup white rum or Cointreau, Kirsch, Grand
   Marnier, or Cognac
1 cup raspberries
¾ cup semolina flour
¾ cup all-purpose flour
1 cup crème fraîche, to serve

Preheat the oven to 375°F.

Slice the apples into quarters and core. Cut the quarters into ¼-inch-thick slices. In a large saucepan over medium heat, melt 1 tablespoon of the butter. Add the apples and cook, stirring occasionally, for 10 minutes, or until they are soft. Add the raisins, ½ cup of the brown sugar, the vanilla extract, and cinnamon and stir to combine. Increase the heat to high and add the rum. Flame the alcohol by touching it with a lit match and cook until the flame is extinguished. Pour the apple mixture into a 3-quart baking dish and sprinkle with the raspberries. Set aside.

In a medium mixing bowl, combine the semolina and all-purpose flours, the remaining 1½ cups of brown sugar, and the remaining ¼ cup of butter. Work the butter into the flour using your fingertips until the mixture is crumbly. Spread the crumbs over the apple mixture and bake for 30 minutes, or until the crumble is golden brown and the mixture is bubbly. Serve warm with a dollop of crème fraîche.

THE FRUIT CRUMBLE.

ISABELLE, BEFORE THE HUNT.

ABOVE: TWO GENERATIONS. BELOW: THE PERFECT DECOY!

ABOVE: BACK FROM THE HUNT. BELOW: LA RENAUDIÈRE.

KEPT CLOSE TO THE TREES FOR PROTECTION.

A COLORFUL GUESTROOM.

GERARD HAS BEEN WITH ISABELLE FOR YEARS.

SERIOUS PURSUITS BY DAY, GAMES BY EVENING.

Cocktails on the Canal

WITH LARRY LOVETT

Larry Lovett may well be the most famous American living in Venice, and understandably so. For many years, he worked with various private committees to conserve Venice's art and architecture. He recently founded Venetian Heritage, an organization dedicated to the preservation of the Venetian empire.

But that's not his only contribution to the City of Dreams. In Venice, Larry is a modern-day Henry James figure come to life, hosting nights of exquisite music, fine cuisine, and candlelit conversation at his majestic apartment on the Grand Canal.

Cocktails on Larry's terrace at sunset conjure up all the romance and fantasy that are synonymous with Venice. The terrace overlooks the Rialto bridge and a beautiful sixteenth-century San Sovino building that used to house Venice's wholesale vegetable market. With this setting as our backdrop, we

Mr. Laurence Lovett

BELLINIS

TUNA TARTARE

CROQUE MONSIEUR

<small>ALL RECIPES COURTESY OF HARRY'S BAR</small>

feasted on tuna tartare, salmon croquettes, and croque monsieur sandwiches. These treats were washed down with Bellinis—a mixture of champagne and peach nectar, and the signature drink of Harry's Bar, a Venetian institution. In fact, when Larry is not entertaining at home, it's his canteen.

Larry has restored his apartment, part of what was once a private nineteenth-century palazzo, so beautifully that it is now one of the most splendid houses on the Grand Canal. And when he entertains he matches its brilliance. For his table settings, he creates an atmosphere of quiet grandeur. His favorite china is Limoges, circa 1880, which he bought years ago because it had his initials on the plates in big, fancy letters. "I have eighteen plates for each course and it's very gilded, dressy, and grand," he admits, "with beautiful painted pictures of stags, boars, and forests. The fish plates have mountain streams, fish jumping, and seascapes."

Larry describes the way he entertains as slightly stuffy, but basically lighthearted. As far as I'm concerned, apart from the Limoges there is nothing stuffy about his dinners or lunches. As for lighthearted, he's on the mark. His own exuberance creates an atmosphere of goodwill and high spirits. Larry's appreciation for beauty, so evident in everything he does, extends to his guest list and he enjoys having attractive people at his table. Not beautiful, necessarily, he says, but well groomed and dressed to the best of their

abilities. Few would admit to that for fear of sounding shallow, but I think it's true of most people who entertain and I admire Larry for his candor. "I also want guests of good character," he says. "I hope you won't meet any bums at my house, even if they are rich or famous. Of course I do like agreeable conversation— brilliant when possible."

Bellinis

Made with the delicate rose-colored essence of white peaches and mixed with Prosecco, the Italian version of champagne that comes from around Treviso, the Bellini is a salute to the tradition of Harry's Bar, since it was created by his father in the 1930s and christened in honor of the Giovanni Bellini exposition in Venice in 1948.

SERVES 2

2 ounces peach purée
6 ounces very cold Prosecco

Mix the purée and wine together in a cocktail shaker and pour into chilled glasses to serve.

Tuna Tartare

Be sure to use only the very best quality tuna for these fresh-tasting canapés. If you prefer, serve scoops of the tuna on tuiles made by baking 2-inch rounds of grated Parmesan on a baking sheet in a 400°F oven for 3 or 4 minutes. Cool on the sheets for a minute, then use a spatula to remove the tuiles and drape over a rolling pin to create a curved shape.

SERVES 6

12 ounces sashimi-quality tuna, finely diced
  by hand
1 small red onion, very finely diced
1 teaspoon finely grated lime zest
2 tablespoons extra-virgin olive oil
Salt and freshly ground black pepper to taste
1 cucumber, scrubbed
12 thin strips lime zest for garnish

Combine the tuna, onion, lime zest, and olive oil in a medium bowl and mix gently. Season with salt and pepper.

Cut the cucumber into ½-inch-thick slices. Scoop out most of the center with a spoon, making an indentation. Spoon a heaping teaspoonful of the tuna mixture onto each cucumber slice, and then garnish with strips of lime. Serve immediately.

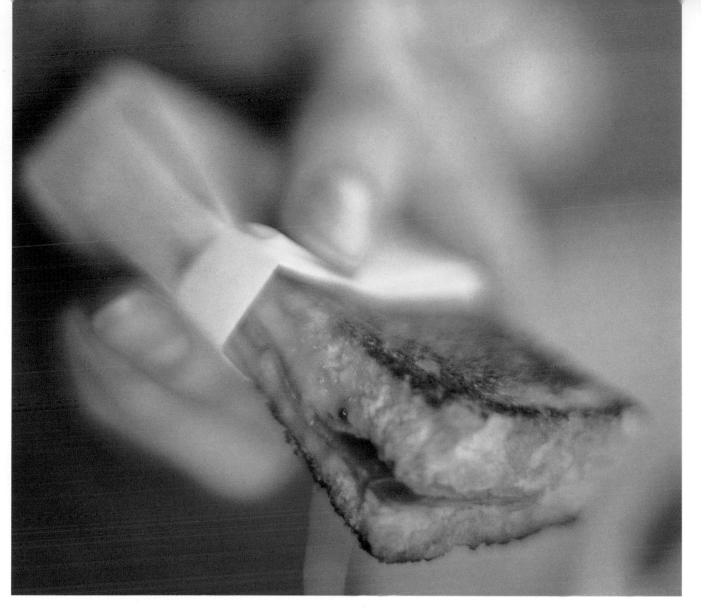

Croque Monsieur

Fried in olive oil, this classic adaptation of a French favorite makes an irresistible nibble when the hot strips are passed wrapped in crisp paper napkins.

MAKES 6 SANDWICHES

½ pound Gruyère or Emmentaler cheese, diced
1 large egg yolk
1 tablespoon Worcestershire sauce
1 teaspoon Dijon mustard
⅛ teaspoon cayenne pepper
Salt to taste
2 to 3 tablespoons heavy cream, as needed
12 thin slices good-quality white bread, crusts removed
¼ pound sliced smoked ham
Olive oil for frying

In the bowl of a food processor, combine the cheese, egg yolk, Worcestershire sauce, mustard, and cayenne and process until smooth. Season with salt. If the mixture is too thick to spread easily, thin it with a little cream.

Spread the cheese mixture over one side of each bread slice. Arrange the ham over the cheese on half the pieces of bread and top with the remaining bread slices. Press the sandwiches together firmly.

Heat a scant tablespoon of oil in a heavy skillet over medium-high heat until very hot. Add as many sandwiches as will fit in the pan and fry, turning once, until they are golden brown and crisp. Repeat with the remaining sandwiches, adding more oil to the pan as necessary. Cut the sandwiches in half and serve hot, wrapped in a paper napkin.

Buffets

& Galas

The David-Weills'
Riviera Retreat

If I were asked what is the most luxurious experience in my life, I would say a weekend with Hélène and Michel David-Weill at their villa on the Mediterranean. Every detail is perfectly thought out, and lavish attention and beautiful surroundings spoil Hélène and Michel's guests.

Monsieur and Madame Michel David-Weill

MONKFISH-STUFFED
ZUCCHINI FLOWERS

CHICKEN "CHAUD-FROID"

LAMB CURRY

RICE PILAF

FIG SORBET WITH "QUEEN OF SABA" CHOCOLATE COOKIES

CHEF DE CUISINE: JÉRÔME BUTEL

The house has been in the David-Weill family for two generations. It's steeped in tradition and a weekend there is like a fairy tale from a past way of life. The enchantment begins with the guest bedrooms. Every detail gives pleasure to the senses, from linen sheets to blanket covers to the fluffiest of towels I've ever used. Each morning a tray is brought to your room with an embroidered cloth, fresh linens, and a tiny vase of flowers, all matching the colors of your bedroom. The tray is laden with homemade brioches, croissants, jams, and fruits so beautiful they look artificial.

There are usually a dozen houseguests at any time during the summer and a large domestic staff to see to the guests' every need, but there is no major domo. Hélène runs her house and every detail is masterminded by her. Though she has a world-class chef, she's in conference with him every morning to plan the meals of the day.

The David-Weills entertain with a relaxed formality. Dinner is served at the table, lunch is also seated but a buffet, and place cards are never used. Instead, Hélène and Michel direct where each guest will sit in such a comfortable way that it seems as if the decision of placement is a spontaneous one.

For my visit, there were twenty of us, and the buffet lunch was a cornucopia of mouthwatering dishes. Space has not allowed me to share the entire menu. In addition to the recipes I've included, there were cold salads indigenous to the region, hot dishes, boeuf en gelée—a David-Weill house specialty—

and a variety of artisanal cheeses. Every platter is a temptation as well as a work of art. Presentation is a signature of the David-Weill style of entertaining. Hélène's chef de cuisine, Jérôme Butel, and his assistants are artists in the kitchen and strive to make the food as decorative as it is edible. The buffet table is arranged like a beautiful still life. The architectural centerpiece of this meal was a pyramid of shrimp that was twelve and a half inches high.

Amid this artful display there is an informal quality. Lunches are served on a terrace that overlooks the Mediterranean. When it's time to eat, most of the guests have been sunbathing down at the David-Weills' private beach, so the dress code is bathing suits and sarongs.

Michel is the chairman of Lazard Frères, the venerable investment-banking firm. Together he and Hélène are renowned patrons of the arts. Their remarkable summer house-party weekends reflect the range of their interests. They seamlessly blend leaders in the worlds of arts and letters, politics, and finance, as well as family, children, and grandchildren and devoted friends. Whether it's lunch or dinner, fascinating conversation, be it artistic, financial, political, or just juicy gossip, is always at its apex at the David-Weills'. The diversity of menu and guests makes for a weekend that I look forward to each summer and that, after nearly four decades, is still unrivaled.

gently mix to combine. Place the mixture in a resealable plastic bag and snip off one corner.

Fill each flower loosely with stuffing and place on a lightly greased baking sheet. Drizzle with a little of the olive oil and bake for 20 minutes, or until the filling has set.

Chicken "Chaud-Froid"

This classic and very decorative cold dish is garnished here with fine slices of truffle, but a sprinkling of fresh herbs such as tarragon is delicious, too.
SERVES 8 TO 10

3 quarts well-flavored chicken stock
Salt and freshly ground black pepper to taste
1 large roasting chicken (about 5½ pounds)
3 envelopes unflavored powdered gelatin
2 egg yolks, lightly beaten
¼ cup crème fraîche or sour cream
1 small black truffle (optional), thinly sliced

In a large pot, bring the stock to a simmer over low heat. Season with salt and pepper, add the chicken, and poach uncovered for 1½ hours, or until the juices run clear when the thigh is pierced with a fork. Transfer the chicken to a rack. When it is cool enough to handle, remove the skin and cut the chicken into 10 serving pieces. Cover and refrigerate until chilled.

Skim the fat from the stock and bring it to a boil. Sprinkle in 2 envelopes of the gelatin and remove from the heat, stirring until it thickens. Combine the egg yolks and the crème fraîche in a small mixing bowl and slowly whisk the mixture into the stock. Strain the thickened liquid through a fine sieve and allow to cool.

Arrange the chicken on a large serving platter. Ladle the cooled liquid over the chicken, taking care to cover each piece evenly; they should have a thick, opaque covering. Place a slice of truffle, if using, on each chicken piece.

Sprinkle the remaining envelope of gelatin into 1 cup of cold water and stir to dissolve; let stand for 1 minute. Add 1 cup of hot water and stir until the gelatin is completely dissolved. Using a pastry brush, glaze each chicken piece with a thin coating of gelatin. Refrigerate for 1 hour before serving.

Monkfish-Stuffed Zucchini Flowers

Serve straight from the oven to prevent the flowers from becoming soft.
SERVES 8

16 zucchini blossoms
1½ pounds monkfish
3 egg whites
¼ cup crème fraîche or sour cream
¼ cup chopped fresh chives
¼ cup finely chopped red bell pepper
2 tablespoons olive oil

Preheat the oven to 300°F.

Gently open up the zucchini flowers and remove the stamens; set aside. Place the monkfish in the bowl of a food processor and pulse until it is finely chopped. Transfer to a medium mixing bowl. Add the egg whites and crème fraîche and mix well, then add the chives and bell pepper and

Heat 1 tablespoon of the olive oil in a large sauté pan over high heat. Cook the lamb in 4 batches using 1 tablespoon of oil for each; cook for 10 minutes, or until browned on all sides. Remove the meat from the pan and set aside.

Reduce the heat to medium, add the onion, and cook for 5 minutes, until golden. Add the curry powder, cumin, cinnamon, salt, and pepper and cook for 1 minute, stirring occasionally, until aromatic. Add the apples, bananas, apricots, and lemon, reduce the heat to low, and cook gently for 30 minutes, until the fruit is very soft.

Return the lamb to the pan and add the coconut milk. Simmer gently for 1 hour, or until the lamb is tender.

Rice Pilaf

SERVES 8 TO 10

3 cups basmati rice
2 tablespoons olive oil
½ cup minced red bell pepper
½ cup golden raisins
½ cup chopped blanched almonds

Rinse the rice in a strainer under running water and drain well.

Heat the olive oil in a large, heavy saucepan over medium heat and add the rice. Cook, stirring, until the oil is absorbed and the rice begins to turn golden brown, about 3 minutes. Add 6 cups of water, increase the heat to high, and bring to a boil. Cover with a tight-fitting lid, reduce the heat to low, and simmer for 20 minutes, until all the water is absorbed.

When the rice is tender, stir in the bell pepper, raisins, and almonds. Cover and allow to stand for 5 minutes before serving.

Lamb Curry

A fruit base makes this curry very mild yet rich and flavorful. Garnish with grated apple and shredded coconut and serve with mango chutney.

SERVES 8 TO 10

4 tablespoons olive oil
1 whole boned leg of lamb (about 5 pounds), trimmed and cut into 1-inch cubes
1 large onion, chopped
2 tablespoons curry powder
½ teaspoon ground cumin
1 teaspoon ground cinnamon
Salt and freshly ground black pepper to taste
5 apples, peeled, cored, and cut into ½-inch cubes
3 bananas, thinly sliced
4 apricots, chopped
1 lemon, peeled, seeded, and chopped
3 cups unsweetened coconut milk

Fig Sorbet

The delicate fig sorbet is wonderfully refreshing served with rich chocolate cookies.

SERVES 8

24 large ripe purple figs
Juice of 2 lemons
1¼ cups sugar
¼ cup heavy cream

Peel the figs, place in a shallow dish, and pour the lemon juice over them. Pass the figs through a food mill using the middle-size screen into a medium bowl, or process until coarsely puréed in a food processor; you should have about 2 cups of purée. Mix the puréed figs with the sugar and add the cream, stirring to combine. Spoon the purée into the container of an ice-cream maker and freeze according to the manufacturer's instructions.

"Queen of Saba" Chocolate Cookies

MAKES 8 TO 10 COOKIES

5 ounces bittersweet chocolate, chopped
1 tablespoon strong coffee or espresso
½ cup (1 stick) unsalted butter
3 eggs, separated
1 cup confectioners' sugar
½ cup sifted all-purpose flour

Preheat the oven to 350°F. Line a baking sheet with parchment paper.

Combine the chocolate, coffee, and butter in the top of a double boiler or a stainless-steel bowl. Set over a pot of simmering water until melted, stirring occasionally with a wooden spoon. Remove from the heat and set aside until lukewarm.

In a large bowl, combine the egg yolks and confectioners' sugar and beat until pale yellow in color, about 5 minutes. Gently stir in the sifted flour, using a whisk. Slowly pour the chocolate mixture into the egg-yolk mixture and gently stir to combine.

In a medium bowl, beat the egg whites until they form stiff peaks, about 5 minutes. Gently fold them into the chocolate mixture until well combined.

Gently pour the batter onto the prepared baking sheet and spread with a spatula into a ½-inch-thick rectangle, 12 inches long by 8 inches wide. Bake for 12 minutes, or until a toothpick inserted into the center comes out clean. Transfer to a rack to cool.

Using a sharp knife, cut the sheet into triangles, or any other desired shape. Serve with a scoop of sorbet on each.

Big Barbecue

at the Wyatt Ranch

Lynn Wyatt is the Yellow Rose of Texas. Her personality is bigger than life; her generosity equals the Lone Star State in size. Whether it's her dinner or someone else's, a seat next to Lynn is the "A" seat. She has a way of charming and enchanting anyone. Whether it's Houston or her villa on the Côte d'Azur or down home at Tasajillo—the ranch she and her husband, Oscar, maintain in South Texas— no one turns down an invitation from Lynn.

Mr. and Mrs. Oscar Wyatt

FROZEN MARGARITAS

GUACAMOLE

BARBECUED CHICKEN PIECES

GRILLED VEGETABLES

MEXICAN RICE

BEEF FAJITAS

LEMON MERINGUE PIE

CHEF: JEAN TOMMY MEIZE

If I had to name the traits that make Lynn the haute hostess that she is, I would say her warmth and her desire to make everyone happy. And she derives such pleasure from entertaining that it's contagious. In Houston, she's like a clearinghouse: anyone who's passing through calls her and she says "Come on over."

I know many people who have style, but few who exude glamour the way Lynn does—the word was invented for her. She's more of a movie star than a movie star and this innate style extends into everything she does. Like a great star, she's a chameleon and so her parties are often a reflection of her penchant for the dramatic, with themes ranging from Gypsy to safari.

Of course, at Tasajillo Lynn doesn't need a theme; the ranch is the theme. Being at Tasajillo is like stepping onto the set of a John Ford western. And when Lynn decides to give a backyard barbecue, neighbors from miles around stop their quail shooting to come for lunch.

For my visit, Lynn pulled out all the stops and laid on guacamole, grilled vegetables, beef fajitas, Mexican rice, margaritas, and a Mariachi band. If that's not Texas-style hospitality, then what is?

When Lynn has weekend guests at the ranch, she tries to serve each meal in a different setting. Dinner is usually in the wine cellar or dining room. Lunch is taken on the terrace overlooking the pool. Barbecue picnics take place in a gazebo at the lake on their property. She knows her guests are hoping for

a real ranch-style lunch at least once during their stay, so she makes that the grand finale. The Wyatts' French chef, who travels between their three houses, is full of imaginative ideas and adapts his menus to the location; he's learned to cook Tex-Mex food like a native. "There's always a sprinkling of Texas ranch-style tastes," says Lynn, "mixed with French food." A mesquite-grilled baby pig will be paired with purée of French seeded home-grown carrots or other fresh garden vegetables.

Though Lynn likes to satisfy her guests' craving for ranch-style cooking, there's another overriding signature to all the food she serves in her houses: Lynn is very health-conscious. She exercises religiously and watches what she eats. She likes to keep the cholesterol count down, so things are less on the creamy side. At lunch and dinner there's generally an emphasis on leafy vegetables and fruit.

To entertain on the scale that Lynn does requires more than just star quality. Like a conscientious producer or director, she oversees every detail in advance, so that by the time the guests arrive she can relax and enjoy the show. The seating plan is her priority. You can have the most beautiful surroundings and the greatest food in the world, but if the guests aren't stimulated, the party won't be a success. "When a guest says to me after dinner," Lynn observes, "that his or her table had the most lively conversation and another tells me his or her table was the most fun, I know my efforts have paid off."

Guacamole

The only way to keep guacamole fresh is to make only what you can eat right away. Tommy served these in individual portions, great for a party.

SERVES 8

4 ripe avocados, halved and pitted
Juice of 4 limes
½ teaspoon ground cumin
1 fresh jalapeño pepper, seeds removed and finely chopped
Dried ground cayenne pepper to taste
Lemon pepper to taste
8 cups tortilla chips

Halve the avocados and scoop the flesh into a medium mixing bowl, reserving the skins. Add the lime juice and cumin and, with a fork, mash the avocado to a smooth consistency. Add the chopped jalapeño and stir to combine. Season with cayenne and lemon pepper.

Spoon the guacamole back into the 8 reserved avocado shells and arrange on a platter with tortilla chips or serve each portion individually.

Barbecued Chicken Pieces

SERVES 8

1 tablespoon salt
1 tablespoon paprika
1 tablespoon sugar
1 tablespoon dry mustard powder
1 tablespoon lemon pepper
1 tablespoon cayenne pepper
1 tablespoon garlic powder
16 chicken leg and thigh pieces
1 cup Barbecue Sauce (recipe follows)

In a medium mixing bowl, combine the salt, paprika, sugar, mustard powder, lemon pepper, cayenne pepper, and garlic powder and mix well. Rub the mixture over the chicken pieces, place the pieces in a glass or ceramic dish, cover with plastic wrap, and refrigerate for 1 hour.

Prepare a charcoal fire. Cook the chicken pieces for 30 minutes, turning to brown on both sides. Brush the chicken with the barbecue sauce and continue to cook for 10 minutes longer, or until cooked through and golden.

BARBECUE SAUCE

This spicy sauce keeps well and adds punch to any barbecued meat.

MAKES 2 CUPS

1 onion, peeled and coarsely grated
1 teaspoon dry mustard powder
1 teaspoon chili powder
1 teaspoon dried garlic powder
1 teaspoon ground cumin
¼ cup Worcestershire sauce
2 bay leaves
1 cup ketchup
2 tablespoons packed brown sugar
1½ cups beer
2 cups chicken broth
¼ cup white vinegar
Tabasco sauce to taste
Salt and freshly ground black pepper to taste

In a large heavy saucepan, combine the onion, mustard powder, chili powder, garlic powder, cumin, and Worcestershire. Stir to combine and bring to a simmer over medium heat. Cook for 3 minutes, then add the bay leaves, ketchup, brown sugar, beer, chicken broth, and vinegar and mix well.

Increase the heat to high and bring to a boil. Boil for 2 minutes, then reduce the heat to medium-low and simmer for 30 to 45 minutes, until the mixture is quite thick. Season with Tabasco sauce, salt, and pepper.

Remove from the heat and allow to cool. Store the sauce in an airtight jar in the refrigerator for up to 2 weeks.

Grilled Vegetables

SERVES 8

3 zucchini, sliced into ¼-inch diagonal slices
2 medium eggplants, peeled and sliced into
    ¼-inch rounds
2 red bell peppers, halved, seeded, and sliced into
    1½-inch pieces
2 yellow bell peppers, halved, seeded, and sliced
    into 1½-inch pieces
½ cup extra-virgin olive oil
Salt and freshly ground black pepper to taste

Prepare a charcoal fire. Place the zucchini, eggplant, and peppers in a medium dish and pour over the olive oil. Gently toss the vegetables to coat. Season with salt and pepper. Grill the vegetables in a single layer, turning regularly until tender, about 20 minutes.

Mexican Rice

In Mexican cooking, rice is sautéed in oil with spices before the liquid is added. This enhances the flavor and keeps the kernels from sticking together. You can substitute basmati or long-grain white rice for the Texmati rice.

SERVES 8

3 cups Texmati rice
¼ cup olive oil
5 garlic cloves, chopped
2 onions, diced
3 serrano chilies, stemmed and minced
3 bay leaves
3 tomatoes, diced
2 tablespoons unsalted butter
Salt to taste

Place the rice in a sieve and rinse under cold water for 2 minutes. In a large saucepan, heat the oil over medium heat. Add the garlic, onions, chilies, and rice and sauté for 8 to 10 minutes, or until the rice becomes opaque.

Add 6 cups of water, the bay leaves, tomatoes, butter, and salt and bring to a boil. Reduce the heat to low, cover with a tight-fitting lid, and cook for 20 minutes, or until the liquid is absorbed and the rice is tender.

Beef Fajitas

SERVES 8

Fajitas are simple and fun. Serve with salsa, sour cream, grated cheese, shredded lettuce, and picante sauce so guests can "roll their own."

MAKES 8

1½ pounds skirt steak
1 cup Barbecue Sauce (page 162)
Salt to taste
8 flour tortillas, warmed

Using a sharp knife, butterfly each skirt steak by slicing it in half lengthwise so that the two halves are barely joined. Place the meat in a glass bowl, add the barbecue sauce, and turn to coat well. Cover and marinate for 3 hours in the refrigerator.

Prepare a charcoal fire. Remove the meat from the marinade and season with salt. Discard the marinade. Grill the meat, turning frequently, for 15 minutes, until well done. Transfer to a cutting board and chop into small pieces.

To serve, place on a platter with the tortillas and condiments of choice.

Lemon Meringue Pie

This pie is a true favorite. It can be refrigerated uncovered for 2 days before serving.

SERVES 8 TO 10

Basic Pie Dough (recipe follows)
1¾ cups sugar
6 tablespoons cornstarch
½ cup fresh lemon juice
6 large whole eggs, separated
¼ teaspoon salt
2 tablespoons finely grated lemon zest
4 tablespoons unsalted butter
2 large egg whites
¼ teaspoon cream of tartar

Preheat the oven to 400°F.

On a lightly floured surface, roll out the dough to a 12-inch circle, ⅛ inch thick. Transfer the pastry to a 9-inch pie pan and crimp the edges. Refrigerate for 30 minutes until firm. Line the pie with parchment paper and fill with dry beans. Bake for 20 minutes, or until golden brown. Transfer the pie shell to a wire rack, remove the paper and beans, and allow to cool.

In a medium bowl, combine 1 cup of the sugar and the cornstarch and gradually whisk in 1 cup of water until smooth; set aside.

In a heavy, nonreactive saucepan over medium heat, combine the lemon juice, egg yolks, and salt. Stir in the cornstarch mixture and cook, stirring constantly, until the mixture comes to a boil, about 10 minutes. Remove from the heat and stir in the lemon zest and butter. Pour the filling into the cooled pie crust, cover with plastic wrap, and refrigerate until firm.

Preheat the broiler.

Combine all 8 egg whites, the remaining ¾ cup sugar, and the cream of tartar in the heat-proof bowl of an electric mixer, rest the bowl over a saucepan of simmering water, and whisk until the sugar has dissolved, about 4 minutes. Remove from the heat and beat the mixture until stiff peaks form. Spread the meringue over the pie, starting from the outside edge and covering the entire filling and overlapping the crust.

Place the pie under the broiler and brown the meringue for 25 to 35 seconds, watching carefully to prevent burning, until golden. Cool to room temperature on a wire rack before serving.

BASIC PIE DOUGH

1¼ cups all-purpose flour
½ teaspoon salt
1 teaspoon sugar
½ cup (1 stick) unsalted butter, chilled and cut into pieces
1 teaspoon cider vinegar

Place the flour, salt, and sugar in the bowl of a food processor with the metal blade and pulse to combine. Add the butter and pulse until the mixture resembles coarse meal. Add 3 tablespoons of ice water and the vinegar in a slow, steady stream while pulsing, until the crumbs hold together when squeezed. If necessary, add more ice water, 1 teaspoon at a time.

Form the dough into a disk, cover with plastic wrap, and refrigerate for 1 to 2 hours.

Being at Tasajillo is like stepping onto the set of a John Ford western.

THE LORD OF THE MANOR.

MY GUEST SUITE—WHY DID I EVER LEAVE?

LYNNE SAYS, "IF YOU DON'T LIKE THE WEATHER, WAIT A MINUTE!"

IT'S HUMBLE, BUT IT'S HOME.

BOOTED TO GO.

Artful
Organics
at Casa Bowes

Frances Bowes and I are sandbox friends. We grew up together in San Francisco and the friendship has lasted so long that I feel she's a part of my life and I'm a part of hers. Though she has an apartment in New York, I love to visit her on her home turf. We always have a million things to talk about. Like me, she's outspoken and always says what's on her mind. John is her perfect complement, and they are one of the few couples I know that have been married as long as Tommy and I have.

Mr. and Mrs. John Bowes

HARICOTS VERTS WITH
TARRAGON VINAIGRETTE

ORANGE-GINGER
ROASTED BEETS

TOMATO AND GOAT CHEESE TART
WITH TAPENADE

CUCUMBERS IN MINT
CRÈME FRAÎCHE

COLD POACHED SALMON
ON ARUGULA WITH SAUCE VERTE AND
ORANGE-BASIL VINAIGRETTE

SOURDOUGH ROLLS

ASSORTED SORBETS
WITH FRESH BERRIES
AND COOKIES

CHEF: KATE KINNEY

She and her husband, John, are patrons and leaders in the world of contemporary art. Since the 1960s they have lived with works of art by painters and sculptors who epitomize and have shaped the modern art movement. Four years ago, they commissioned the Mexican architect Ricardo Legorreta to design a house for them on four hundred acres of former ranchland in the Sonoma Valley. Today it is a stunning show-case for their art collection and an ideal space for entertaining.

The trip up to the house is a hallucinatory experience. You drive past some of California's best winer-ies before entering a long, winding road that continues past farm buildings and old farmhouses until, suddenly, contemporary sculptures appear out of nowhere. Beyond the sculptures, sitting on a ridge over-looking the valley, are a group of terra-cotta-colored pavilions linked by corridors and entered through a forty-eight-foot-high tower. This rambling, postmodern house is Casa Bowes.

The house was originally conceived to accommodate their large-scale art collection, but John and Frances now realize it's become a center for their family that includes three grown children and grand-children. Frances grew up in family compounds, and Casa Bowes has followed in that tradition. When I visited, the house was filled with friends, neighbors, and family ranging in age from three on up.

The house is furnished with an uncanny eye for proportion. Frances approaches her menus the same

way: they are always first-rate and uncomplicated. When you live in California you're spoiled by the ready availability of fresh produce, and Sonoma is the state's heartland of great fruit and vegetables. Our lunch was a perfect example of what Frances likes to serve. A huge fish is always on the menu. There's always a hot dish even in summer and the menu is filled out with a variety of vegetable dishes prepared with light and refreshing combinations of spices and sauce variations. Frances is fond of what she calls "straight food." "It's what my mother had," she says. "So I like to have lots of asparagus, artichokes, and dishes like corn pudding. Sometimes, though, when I inflict my mother's recipes on guests, they don't get it. I remember once serving a huge head of cauliflower with caper butter sauce, which is one of my favorites. My guests were completely lost with that one."

Lunches and dinners are served buffet style but always seated. And rather than an oversized dining table, Frances prefers a long, narrow table with everyone jammed in close, so that there's a family conviviality to the meals.

Despite the rooms' starkness and the spatial grandeur of the soaring space, there are no jarring notes at Casa Bowes. Instead, it's comfortable and welcoming. No architect in the world can design that feeling. For those features, John and Frances are their own architects.

FRANCIS AND JOHN SHARE A TANGO IN THE AFTERNOON.

A SCALE MODEL OF CASA BOWES IN SILVER.

A PERIDOT AND A ZEBRA TOMATO.

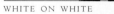

WHITE ON WHITE

ABOVE: THE TOMATO TART. BELOW: DAISY PLAYS DRESS-UP.

Frances prefers a long narrow table with everyone jammed in close, so that there's a **family conviviality** to the meals.

Haricots Verts with Tarragon Vinaigrette

Recipe by Kate Kinney.

SERVES 30 AS PART OF A BUFFET

3 shallots, finely diced
1 cup fresh tarragon leaves, finely chopped
1 teaspoon plus 2 tablespoons kosher salt
½ teaspoon freshly ground black pepper
½ cup mild vinegar, such as champagne vinegar
2 teaspoons Dijon mustard
1½ to 2 cups extra-virgin olive oil
5 pounds organic haricots verts or small green
   beans, stem ends removed
1 organic red onion, cut into thin lengthwise
   julienne slices
1 pint organic cherry and golden tomatoes, halved

In a large salad bowl, combine the shallots, tarragon, the 1 teaspoon of salt, the pepper, and vinegar. Allow to stand for 30 minutes.

Whisk in the mustard, then slowly pour in the olive oil, whisking constantly to emulsify. Set aside 2 tablespoons of the vinaigrette.

Fill a large saucepan halfway with water and bring to a boil. Add the 2 tablespoons of salt and the beans and cook for 3 minutes, or until the beans are just tender.

Drain the beans and place them on a clean kitchen towel to blot any excess water. While the beans are still warm, add them to the vinaigrette and toss. Marinate at room temperature for 30 minutes.

Place the onion slices in a small strainer and submerge the strainer in a bowl of ice water for 30 minutes. Drain the onions and blot on paper towels.

Toss the tomatoes and onion with the reserved 2 tablespoons of vinaigrette and scatter over the beans.

Orange-Ginger Roasted Beets

The beets are best prepared one day in advance to allow flavors to develop fully. Use a citrus zester to make attractive thin strips of zest that add flavor to the beets. Recipe by Kate Kinney.

SERVES 30 AS PART OF A BUFFET

3 pounds small, organic red beets
3 pounds small, organic yellow or orange beets
¼ pound fresh organic ginger
2 quarts fresh orange juice
2 teaspoons kosher salt
1 teaspoon freshly ground black pepper
Finely julienned zest of 8 oranges

Preheat the oven to 450°F.

Remove the beet greens, leaving ½ inch of stem attached. Do not cut the root end. Wash the beets and, keeping the red and yellow beets separate, wrap the beets in aluminum foil, grouping 6 beets in each packet.

Place the foil packets on baking sheets and roast for 20 to 45 minutes, or until a paring knife or skewer easily pierces the beets. (Gold beets tend to cook more quickly, so start checking after 20 minutes.) Carefully open the foil and allow the beets to cool slightly.

Meanwhile, peel the ginger and cut it into ½-inch slices. Smash with the side of a heavy knife or cleaver and then mince. In a large bowl, combine the ginger, orange juice, salt, and pepper.

Slip the skins off the beets and trim the root and stem ends. Cut the beets in half lengthwise, then cut each half into 4 lengthwise half moons.

While the beets are still warm, combine them with the orange-ginger marinade. Refrigerate for 12 to 24 hours, tossing occasionally.

To serve, drain the beets, place on a serving platter, and garnish with the orange zest.

Tomato and Goat Cheese Tart with Tapenade

Earthy tapenade, a pungent blend of olives, capers, and anchovies, gives this elegant tart a flavor boost. Recipe by Kate Kinney.

SERVES 30 AS PART OF A BUFFET;
12 AS A LUNCHEON ENTRÉE

6 pounds assorted organic tomatoes (preferably heirloom), sliced ⅛ inch thick
Kosher salt

TAPENADE
½ pound pitted kalamata olives
3 tablespoons salt-cured capers, soaked in water for 30 minutes, drained, and patted dry
2 anchovy fillets, soaked in water and patted dry
1 head of organic garlic, cloves separated, peeled, and minced
½ cup extra-virgin olive oil
1 tablespoon fresh lemon juice
Freshly ground black pepper to taste

2 pounds creamy goat cheese
1 bunch of organic fresh basil, half chopped and half chiffonade (cut into fine ribbons)
3 pounds frozen puff pastry, thawed for 45 minutes

Lightly sprinkle the tomato slices with the salt and drain on paper towels for 2 hours (turn the slices and place on fresh paper towels after 1 hour).

To make the tapenade, combine the olives, capers, and anchovy fillets in a food processor and process until finely chopped. Add half of the garlic, the olive oil, lemon juice, and a few grinds of fresh black pepper. Pulse to combine and transfer to a small bowl.

In the same processor bowl (no need to wash it), purée the goat cheese and the remaining garlic, adding a bit more oil if necessary to create a creamy, smooth texture. Add the chopped basil and pulse just to mix; do not overprocess. Transfer the mixture to a medium bowl.

Preheat the oven to 375°F.

On a lightly floured surface, roll out the thawed puff pastry to a large ¼-inch-thick rectangle. Cut the pastry into two 6-inch-wide strips

(continued on next page)

(length is not important). Lightly spread the goat cheese on both strips of pastry, leaving a ¾-inch border on all sides. Fold over ½-inch edges of the pastry to create a rim. The tarts should have a slightly rustic look.

Place the tarts on 2 ungreased baking trays. Arrange the tomato slices on top of the goat cheese, alternating colors and sizes. Bake the tarts for 15 minutes, or until golden brown. Let the tarts cool slightly, then slide them onto a cutting board. Cut each tart into bite-sized pieces. Arrange on platters and garnish with freshly ground black pepper, a light drizzle of the tapenade, and some basil chiffonade.

Cucumbers in Mint Crème Fraîche

This recipe has been adapted from the California Academy cookbook series. Make it one day in advance.

SERVES 30 AS PART OF A BUFFET

16 large cucumbers
½ cup kosher salt, plus more to taste
1 cup crème fraîche or sour cream
4 shallots, finely diced
½ cup chopped fresh spearmint leaves, plus 4 to 5 leaves cut in chiffonade (cut into fine ribbons)
4 teaspoons freshly ground black pepper
2 tablespoons fresh lemon juice
Finely julienned zest of 2 lemons

Peel the cucumbers and halve them lengthwise. Use a teaspoon to scoop out the seeds, then cut crosswise into ¼-inch slices. In a large bowl,

gently toss the cucumbers with the salt and then place in a nonaluminum strainer or colander and drain for 4 hours.

In a large bowl, combine the crème fraîche, shallots, chopped spearmint, and 3 teaspoons of the pepper. Rinse the cucumbers and pat dry with paper towels. Gently stir the cucumbers into the crème fraîche mixture. Refrigerate for 12 hours.

Before serving, gently stir the fresh lemon juice into the cucumber mixture. Season with salt and garnish with the mint chiffonade, lemon zest, and remaining teaspoon of pepper.

Cold Poached Salmon on Arugula with Sauce Verte and Orange-Basil Vinaigrette

Recipe by Kate Kinney.

SERVES 30 AS PART OF A BUFFET

POACHING LIQUID
2 cups vinegar
2 tablespoons kosher salt
3 yellow onions, sliced
8 sprigs of fresh thyme
4 whole California bay leaves
1 tablespoon whole black peppercorns

One 8- to 10-pound whole fresh salmon (preferably wild Pacific), head and tail intact, cleaned and scales and gills removed
2 pounds baby arugula, spinach, or watercress
2 bunches of radishes, finely sliced
4 cups Orange-Basil Vinaigrette (recipe follows)
4 cups Sauce Verte (recipe follows)

In a large pot, combine 4 quarts of water with the vinegar, salt, onions, thyme, bay leaves, and peppercorns. Place over high heat and bring to a boil. Reduce heat and simmer for 30 minutes. Strain the hot liquid through a sieve and allow to cool slightly.

Measure the girth of the salmon at the thickest part of the body. Place the whole salmon in a fish poacher and add enough lukewarm poaching

(continued on next page)

liquid to cover the fish, topping with water if necessary. Place the poacher over two burners on the stovetop and slowly bring the liquid to a simmer. Cook the salmon for 7 minutes per inch of thickness, until the internal temperature reads 135°F. on a thermometer placed in the thickest part of the flesh. Do not let the temperature of the liquid exceed 200°F. The salmon is cooked when the flesh begins to flake when separated with a fork but still meets with resistance at the bone. Allow the salmon to cool in the poacher for 30 minutes. Carefully remove the salmon and drain. Transfer to a baking sheet lined with plastic wrap, cover with plastic wrap, and refrigerate until chilled.

To serve, use a sharp paring knife to remove the skin and any dark flesh from the top side of the salmon.

Toss the arugula and the radishes with a small amount of the orange-basil vinaigrette and arrange on a large serving platter. While carefully holding the plastic under the salmon, gently invert it onto the platter. Remove the skin and any dark flesh from the second side of the fish. Drizzle the salmon with a little sauce verte, and serve the remaining sauce verte and orange-basil vinaigrette on the side.

SAUCE VERTE

This is a lighter version of the classic mayonnaise-based sauce.
MAKES 4 CUPS

2 shallots, minced
1 teaspoon kosher salt
½ teaspoon freshly ground black pepper
½ cup fresh chervil leaves, minced
½ cup fresh tarragon leaves, minced
½ cup fresh flat-leaf parsley, minced
½ cup champagne vinegar or rice wine vinegar
3 cups mild-flavored extra-virgin olive oil

Combine the shallots, salt, pepper, and herbs with the vinegar and let rest for 30 minutes. Slowly whisk in the olive oil until the mixture thickens and is well combined. Adjust the salt and pepper to taste.

ORANGE-BASIL VINAIGRETTE

MAKES 5 CUPS

1 bunch of organic fresh basil leaves, chopped
1 shallot, minced
Finely julienned zest of 2 oranges
1 tablespoon kosher salt
½ teaspoon freshly ground black pepper
½ cup champagne or rice wine vinegar
2 cups fresh orange juice
2 cups mild extra-virgin olive oil

In a large bowl, combine half of the basil with the shallot, zest, salt, pepper, and vinegar. Let the mixture stand for 30 minutes. Add the orange juice and slowly whisk in the olive oil until the mixture is thoroughly combined. Taste the mixture and adjust the salt and pepper. Just before serving, add the remaining basil and stir gently to combine.

Assorted Sorbets with Fresh Berries

Serve this with mini ginger cookies and small palmiers purchased from a local bakery.

SERVES 30

3 pints organic strawberries
¼ cup superfine sugar
9 pints assorted sorbet, such as lemon, mango, strawberry, or raspberry
3 pints assorted fresh organic berries (red and gold raspberries, marion berries, olallie berries, blackberries, bush berries), washed and picked through

Wash, stem, and quarter the strawberries, place them in a large bowl, and sprinkle lightly with the sugar. Set the strawberries aside to macerate for 1 hour.

Place 3 small scoops of assorted sorbet flavors into individual serving glasses. Top each serving with some of the assorted berries and strawberries, and drizzle with the strawberry juices.

Cocktails
and Buffet
from the Summers

Ann Summers is an unabashed anglophile. Martin Summers is a quintessential Englishman with a hint of Edwardian gentleman, who takes boyish delight in the unexpected. She's quiet and more reserved in temperament, while he's dramatic and openly enthusiastic about everything that fuels his infinite appetite for life. Both have a penchant for the exotic. Twelve years ago, their opposite personalities fused and ignited. Since then, the American beauty and the multitalented Englishman have blended their individualistic styles to create a world of distinctive glamour.

Ann and Martin live in not one but four turn-of-the-century artist's studios in London's Chelsea. Long before they married, Martin bought the derelict buildings, which are hidden from the street by an enclosed courtyard. By interlinking them he

Mr. and Mrs. Martin Summers

LUIZA'S SPECIAL **CHICKEN CURRY**

RAITA

CHOCOLATE BROWNIES

CAIPIRINHA

COOK: LUIZA DE SOOUZE

created large-scaled, classically proportioned rooms that are rare havens of space and sunlight. Above it all, Martin has created a garden stretching one hundred twenty feet across the roof and linked by bridges. It virtually envelopes the house, and the studio skylights provide a stellar view of trees, shrubs, and more than a thousand flowering plants in pots.

By day, Ann is an interior designer at George Spencer, a top decorating firm, and Martin is a partner in LeFevre Gallery, London's leading dealer in Impressionist art. By night, they are one of the supreme party-giving couples in London. An invitation from them is always accompanied by surprises; you never know where or how they might be entertaining. It could be a barbecue in the open air of the roof garden, or a small seated dinner in the main studio room that they've dubbed the "English Room," because virtu-ally everything from the paintings to the furniture is English. Or you might find yourself at a large buffet supper in another room with a Moorish tent, Turkish sofas, Afghan stools, and Bugatti furniture.

Luckily for me, it seems that every time I'm in London, my visit coincides with one of the monthly musical evenings at which students of the Royal Academy of Music entertain. After the music, guests enjoy a buffet dinner of either Chinese or Indian food. Luiza, their longtime Brazilian housekeeper and cook, is a marvel in the kitchen. Over the years she's he's learned to cook Thai, Chinese, and Indian, and then she throws in a little Brazilian for good measure. For our dinner, she whipped up her special chicken curry served with Persian rice.

Ann and Martin's evenings are a joint effort, and their contrasting personalities make for a great team. "Ann is meticulous in organizing and brings precision," offers Martin. "I'm more laissez-faire. As long as the right people are there, I find I'm not bothered if there's a picture light that's burned out."

Luiza's Special Chicken Curry

Luiza de Soouze is originally from Brazil. The curry she has perfected over the past twenty years is famous among the Summers' friends. She cooks the chicken and the sauce separately to prevent the chicken from disintegrating into the curry; the dish is best prepared a day ahead to intensify the flavors. Serve with pappadams, mango chutney, raisins, bananas, raita, and basmati rice.

SERVES 20 TO 30

FOR THE CHICKEN
2 tablespoons salt
2 heaping tablespoons hot Madras curry powder
6 large organic free-range chickens, rinsed

FOR THE CURRY SAUCE
¼ cup vegetable oil
3 onions, chopped
2 tablespoons ground coriander
2 tablespoons ground cumin
2 tablespoons ground cardamom
4 apples, such as Granny Smith or Golden
    Delicious, peeled, cored, and cut into quarters
2 celery stalks, sliced
1½-inch piece fresh ginger, peeled and finely
    sliced
3 carrots, peeled and sliced
1 14-ounce can peeled plum tomatoes
3 ounces tomato paste
15 ounces Patek's mild curry paste
2 heads of crisp head lettuce, cored and sliced
    into ribbons
1 14-ounce can coconut milk

In each of 2 large stockpots, bring 1 gallon of water to a boil. Stir half the salt and half the curry powder into each pot. Add 3 whole chickens to each pot, bring back to the boil, and boil for 40 minutes, or until the chickens are tender and cooked through to the bone. Remove the cooked chickens from the pot, reserving the curried chicken stock separately. Refrigerate the chickens and the stock, covered, overnight.

To make the curry sauce, heat the oil in a very large saucepan over medium-high heat. Add the onions and cook over medium heat for 5 minutes, until translucent. Add the coriander, cumin, and

cardamom and cook the spices, stirring, until very fragrant. Stir in the apples, celery, ginger, carrots, plum tomatoes, tomato paste, and curry paste. Bring the mixture to a boil, then add the lettuce and reduce the heat to low. Simmer for 1½ hours (the lettuce helps to thicken the sauce).

Skim the congealed fat off the stock and strain through a coarse seive. Add the cooked curry sauce to the reserved chicken stock. Bring the mixture to a boil, reduce the heat, and simmer, uncovered, for 7 hours, or until the sauce is reduced by half and the color is a dark chocolate brown. Remove from the heat. When cool, cover and refrigerate overnight to allow the flavors to develop.

The next day, blend the curry sauce, in batches, in a food processor for 1 minute at a time. As each batch is completed, pour the sauce through a fine mesh strainer to remove any vegetables and return to the large pot. When you have strained all the curry sauce, stir in the coconut milk.

Discard the skin and bones from the chickens and cut the meat into ½-inch cubes. Add to the curry sauce and simmer for 30 minutes. Serve.

Raita

SERVES 20

2 cups plain yogurt
2 English cucumbers, peeled and cut into
½-inch cubes
½ teaspoon salt
1 teaspoon ground cumin
½ cup chopped fresh mint leaves

In a large mixing bowl, combine the yogurt, cucumbers, salt, cumin, and mint. Stir gently with a large spoon to combine, cover, and refrigerate until ready to serve.

Chocolate Brownies

MAKES 20

6 ounces bittersweet chocolate, chopped
1 cup (2 sticks) unsalted butter, cut into
8 pieces
4 large eggs
1½ cups dark brown sugar
1 teaspoon vanilla extract
1½ cups all-purpose flour, sifted
½ teaspoon baking powder
1 cup coarsely chopped pecans or walnuts

Preheat the oven to 350°F. Grease a 9 × 12-inch baking pan.

In the top of a double boiler or in a stainless-steel bowl set over a pot of simmering water, combine the chocolate and butter. Stir occasionally with a wooden spoon until the mixture has melted and combined. Remove from the heat and set aside to cool.

In the bowl of an electric mixer fitted with the paddle attachment, beat the eggs, sugar, and vanilla at high speed until the mixture forms very soft peaks. Reduce the speed to low and add the melted chocolate; beat until combined. Slowly add the flour and baking powder, beating until just incorporated. Fold in the nuts and pour the batter into the prepared pan.

Bake for 35 minutes, or until the edges are dry but the center is still soft and a few crumbs stick to a wooden skewer when tested. Remove the pan from the oven and transfer to a wire rack to cool. When cool, invert the brownie onto a rectangular cutting board. Cut the brownie slab into 20 squares. The brownies may be made ahead and stored in an airtight container for up to 2 days.

Caipirinha

Ann and Martin Summers often serve this fabulous Brazilian drink at parties.

SERVES 2

4 ounces Cachaca
3 limes, peeled and diced
3 tablespoons sugar

Place the Cachaca, diced limes, and sugar in a blender. Process until well blended. Pour the mixture through a sieve into chilled glasses.

At Calumet Farm

with the Kwiatkowskis

Henryk de Kwiatkowski is known as the savior of Calumet Farm. For six decades, the farm was a mecca for thoroughbred breeding and racing, breeding nine Kentucky Derby winners. By 1992, however, Calumet was bankrupt and in danger of being shut down. Henryk, a racehorse owner and breeder himself, bought Calumet at auction and has returned the farm to its former glory.

Set on approximately nine hundred acres of white-fenced pastured land, the farm's grand columned manor house had seen better days until Barbara de Kwiatkowski became its chatelaine. Since then, the house has been restored to fabulous condition and decorated with relaxed formality by Barbara and the late, legendary decorator Sister Parish.

Mr. and Mrs. Henryk de Kwiatkowski

SCALLOP AND OYSTER SEVICHE

CHESTNUT-CRUSTED
LOIN OF VENISON

SPICED SWEET POTATO PURÉE WITH A
GINGERBREAD TOPPING

FRANÇOIS PAYARD'S MAKE-AHEAD
CHOCOLATE SOUFFLÉS

BASED ON RECIPES FROM *THE CAFÉ BOULUD
COOKBOOK*, BY DANIEL BOULUD AND DORIE
GREENSPAN, FALL 1999.

Whether at Calumet or at their houses in Greenwich, Connecticut, or in Nassau, the alluring Barbara is a natural hostess. When the fall Breeders' Cup races were held at Lexington's Churchill Downs, Barbara organized a black-tie dinner for fifty guests at Calumet with her usual flair. The evening also honored Brendan Jones, Kentucky's newly elected governor.

We were in Bluegrass country, but the evening had all the glitter and glamour of Versailles created by Barbara with unstudied panache. A string quartet set the stage for a four-course dinner catered by renowned chef Daniel Boulud's firm, Feast & Fêtes, based on recipes from his latest cookbook. The meal started with a seviche of scallops, oysters, and Beluga caviar. That was followed by venison encrusted with chestnuts, and chocolate soufflé. Even in Kentucky, Barbara never serves southern food, nor does she go in for nouvelle cuisine or what she calls "pretty food." She gives her guests what she refers to as "real food." And for her, that's mostly French.

The dinner was served on her favorite new china created by Cindy Sherman, the renowned art photographer. Made in a limited edition in Limoges, the plates feature different images of Sherman herself in the guise of Madame de Pompadour. "I hate a 'perfect table.' I love to have art on the tables," says Barbara. "Like special antique plates or something you don't see everywhere. We have gold racing tropies that I use as underplates and when the china plate is picked up you can see what race it was and who one."

Barbara's inventiveness is what makes even her black-tie dinners relaxed in feeling. She carries that sense of the unexpected through to her eclectic guest lists. She likes to seat unlikely people next to one another, or people who haven't seen one another for a long time. Barbara rarely has a guest of honor and never a theme in mind; she entertains out of sheer enjoyment. "I've never had a bad time at my own party," she told me. "I like to enjoy it as much as, if not more than, everyone else. There's nothing worse than when a hostess is nervous."

Barbara's skill as a hostess supreme is best summed up by one of the extraordinary guests who visited Calumet several years ago. "They should be as proud as we are happy to be here," observed Her Majesty, Queen Elizabeth II.

A GRAND ENTRANCE.

THE FINE DETAILS.

THE HOST AND HOSTESS.

CAVIAR FOR THE SEVICHE.

A CEMETERY FOR CHAMPIONS.

Scallop and Oyster Seviche

Serve the soup in chilled bowls.

SERVES 4

4 very fresh jumbo sea scallops (about 1½ to
  2 ounces each)
Juice of 1 lime
1 lime, zest grated and reserved and flesh peeled
  and cut into small dice
2 teaspoons peeled and finely grated fresh
  horseradish
3 drops of Tabasco sauce
Fleur de sel to taste
16 blue-point or other medium-size briny oysters,
  shucked, liquid reserved
Leaves from one center celery stalk, finely sliced
1 to 2 small round pink radishes, cleaned and
  thinly sliced
1 tablespoon finely chopped fresh chives
2 ounces sevruga or osetra caviar
Freshly ground white pepper to taste
Sliced buttered pumpernickel bread, for serving

Using a sharp, thin knife, cut each scallop crosswise into 5 or 6 slices. In a small mixing bowl,
stir the lime juice, lime zest, horseradish, and
Tabasco sauce together. Add the scallops and turn
them gently in the lime mixture.

As soon as the scallops are moistened, divide
them among 4 chilled bowls, arranging the slices
in an overlapping circle. Sprinkle the scallops
with a bit of fleur de sel. Arrange 4 oysters over
each portion of scallops and top each serving with
an equal amount of celery leaves, radish, diced
lime flesh, and chives; finish with a small spoon-
ful of caviar. Carefully pour a little of the reserved
oyster liquid into each bowl and season with pepper. Serve immediately, passing slices of buttered
pumpernickel.

Chestnut-Crusted Loin of Venison

*The chestnuts for the venison crusts need to be prepared
a day ahead for this recipe.*

SERVES 6

FOR THE CRUST
1¼ pounds chestnuts, shelled and peeled

FOR THE MARINADE
½ cup fresh orange juice
2 tablespoons extra-virgin olive oil
1 teaspoon grated lemon zest
1 teaspoon ground cinnamon
½ teaspoon freshly grated nutmeg
¼ teaspoon ground star anise
¼ teaspoon black peppercorns
2 garlic cloves, peeled and crushed
1 sprig of fresh thyme

2 1½-pound venison loins, trimmed

Salt and freshly ground black pepper to taste

2 large eggs

1 large egg yolk

3 tablespoons all-purpose flour

¼ cup extra-virgin olive oil

1 small shallot, peeled, trimmed, and finely
  chopped

2 teaspoons coarsely crushed black pepper

1 teaspoon grated orange zest

4 teaspoons balsamic vinegar

1 cup red wine

1 teaspoon sugar

1½ cups unsalted beef stock

2 teaspoons unsalted butter

For the crust, break each chestnut into a few pieces and spread the pieces on a baking sheet. Allow the pieces to dry overnight in a warm place —inside the oven with a pilot light is perfect. The next day, place the chestnuts in the work bowl of a food processor and pulse until they break into ¼-inch chunks. Sift the chestnuts, reserving the larger pieces that remain in the

sieve. Transfer these pieces to a plate and set aside.

For the marinade, combine the marinade ingredients with the smaller chestnut pieces in a shallow pan. Add the venison loins and roll in the marinade. Cover the pan tightly with plastic wrap and refrigerate for at least 4 hours, preferably overnight, turning the meat a few times.

For the venison and sauce, center a rack in the oven and preheat the oven to 425°F.

Remove the venison from the marinade, pat the meat dry with paper towels, and season with salt and pepper; discard the marinade. In a pan long enough to accommodate the venison loins, beat together the eggs and yolk. Dust one side of each loin with flour, shake off the excess, and dip that side into the egg mixture and then into the reserved larger chestnuts pieces.

Heat the olive oil in a roasting pan over medium heat. When the oil is hot, add the venison, chestnut-side down, and cook for about 2 minutes, keeping the nut-crusted sides down. Turn the loins over and place the roasting pan in the oven. Roast the venison 10 to 12 minutes, or until medium-rare. Pull the pan from the oven, transfer the loins to a warm platter to rest for about 4 minutes, and make the sauce.

Remove as much grease from the liquid in the roasting pan as possible and then place the pan over medium heat. Add the shallot and cook, stirring, just until translucent. Add the pepper and orange zest, sauté for 1 minute more, and then deglaze the pan with the balsamic vinegar, cooking and stirring until the vinegar just about evaporates. Add the red wine and cook down again until the pan is almost dry. Add the sugar and beef stock and cook at a boil until the liquid is reduced by half. Taste and add salt and pepper as needed. Remove the pan from the heat and swirl the butter into the sauce.

To serve, slice the loins into 12 to 16 slices and serve moistened with sauce and accompanied by spiced sweet potato purée with a gingerbread topping.

Spiced Sweet Potato Purée with a Gingerbread Topping

SERVES 4 TO 6

2 pounds sweet potatoes, peeled and cut into ½-inch cubes
Salt and freshly ground black pepper to taste
1 orange, zest cut into bands, white pith removed, and juiced
2 1½-inch cinnamon sticks
1 bay leaf
1 small onion, peeled
2 cloves
2 tablespoons unsalted butter
1 Golden Delicious apple, peeled, cored, and cut into ¼-inch dice
1 small banana, peeled and sliced ½ inch thick
2 tablespoons sugar
¾ cup heavy cream
¼ cup prepared gingerbread, dried and ground finely like bread crumbs

Preheat the oven to 350°F.

Place the sweet potatoes in a large pot. Add enough water to cover by 1 inch, then add a pinch of salt, half of the orange zest, 1 of the cinnamon sticks, and the bay leaf. Stud the onion with the cloves and add it to the pot. Bring to a boil, lower the heat, and simmer for 20 to 25 minutes, or until the potatoes are fork-tender.

While the sweet potatoes are cooking, prepare the fruit. In a heavy-bottomed pan over medium heat, melt 1 tablespoon of the butter. Add the apple, banana, the remaining orange zest, and the remaining stick of cinnamon and sauté until lightly caramelized, stirring often, 7 to 10 minutes. With a slotted spoon, transfer the fruits to a plate. Add 1 tablespoon of the sugar to the pan, cook to a light brown caramel, carefully add the orange juice, and reduce to 1 tablespoon. Add ¾ of the heavy cream and boil for 3 to 4 minutes. Return the cooked fruit to the pan, mix well, and simmer for 3 to 4 minutes. Remove from the heat and discard the orange zest and cinnamon stick. Keep warm.

When the sweet potatoes are done, drain them well and discard the orange zest, cinnamon stick, bay leaf, and onion. Transfer the warm sweet potatoes to a food processor. Add the fruit, salt, and pepper, and purée. Mix in the remaining cream if the purée is too thick, and taste for seasoning. Transfer the purée to a gratin serving dish and sprinkle with the gingerbread crumbs. Bake in the oven for 15 to 20 minutes, or until the top is light golden brown.

Serve immediately.

François Payard's Make-Ahead Chocolate Soufflés

For this dessert you will need foil, not paper, cupcake liners (the paper liners are not rigid enough to hold their shape once the soufflés begin to rise). Use scissors to trim the cupcake liners to 1½ inches in height.

MAKES 16 SMALL SOUFFLÉS

Nonstick vegetable spray
7 large eggs, separated
⅞ cup sugar
1 tablespoon flour
10 ounces (2½ sticks) unsalted butter
12 ounces Valrhôna bittersweet chocolate, chopped fine
1½ tablespoons lemon juice

Preheat oven to 425°F.

Place 16 foil cupcake liners on a sheet pan. Generously coat the insides of the cups with vegetable spray and set aside.

In a medium bowl, place the egg yolks. In a small bowl, whisk ½ cup of the sugar together with the flour to remove any lumps. Add the flour mixture to the yolks and whisk for 3 min-

(continued on next page)

utes, or until the mixture lightens in color and falls from the whisk in ribbons.

In a small saucepan, melt the butter. Place the chopped chocolate in a large bowl. Pour the hot, bubbling butter over the chocolate and stir with a rubber spatula until melted and smooth.

Place the egg whites, lemon juice, and 2 tablespoons of the sugar in a large bowl. Using an electric mixer set on low speed, beat for 2 minutes. Gradually increase the speed and continue beating for 5 minutes, or until the egg whites are stiff and fluffy. During the last minute of beating, gradually add the remaining ¼ cup of sugar.

Add the egg yolk mixture to the chocolate, and stir until smooth. Fold half of the chocolate mixture into the beaten egg whites with a spatula. Add the remaining chocolate and fold until incorporated and uniformly colored.

Spoon batter evenly into the prepared cupcake liners. Slide the sheet pan into the oven and bake until the soufflés have risen above the rims of the liners, about 7 minutes. Remove the sheet pan from the oven, and cool on a rack until the soufflés are barely warm and slightly deflated, about 15 minutes. Tightly wrap the whole sheet pan with plastic and freeze for at least 1 day and up to 1 month.

About 5 hours before serving, remove the sheet pan from the freezer and let it stand at room temperature.

About 1 hour before serving, preheat the oven to 400°F. Place the sheet pan on top of the warm oven. When ready to bake, unwrap the sheet pan and put it into the oven. Bake on the center rack until the soufflés rise ½ inch above the rims of the cups, about 13 minutes.

Remove the sheet pan from the oven and unmold each soufflé cup onto an individual plate. Serve with ice cream, if desired.

A Birthday Surprise
for Gordon Getty

Gordon Getty is a composer and patron of the musical arts. Ann Getty is a benefactor of literary and artistic pursuits. Several years ago she went back to college, earned a degree in archaeology, and graduated at the top of her class. She's now a regent at the University of California and travels the world taking part in archaeological digs.

Mr. and Mrs. Gordon Getty

BELUGA CAVIAR ON TOAST

RUMAKI

ASSORTED SUSHI

RACK OF LAMB GORDON

JUMBO ASPARAGUS PERSILLÉ

ENDIVE AND WATERCRESS SALAD

BIRTHDAY CAKE

CHEF: ALPHONSE

When the Gettys entertain, their gatherings are more than just parties—they are happenings. And these extravaganzas are often traveling fantasies. For one memorable party in Egypt, Ann invited Cambridge professors and lecturers to be our tour guides as we floated down the Nile. For many years, she hosted a month-long house party in Salzburg for the annual music festival. When Gordon's opera, Plump Jack, was performed in St. Petersburg, they piled friends onto their private plane to share the experience with them.

In San Francisco the Gettys are equally generous hosts. They've been known to lend their house to friends in need of a site to give a dinner, and when Ann and Gordon entertain, they open their doors to everyone they know in San Francisco.

Last December, Ann threw a circus party in honor of Gordon, who was turning sixty-five, and Ivy, their five-year-old granddaughter who shares his birthdate. With two such important guests of honor, Ann pulled out all the stops. The Gettys' Pacific Heights house was transformed into a three-, four-, five-, six-ring circus. Clowns, jugglers, and acrobats greeted us at the door. And that was only the beginning. Sword

swallowers, contortionists, and magicians provided nonstop costumed entertaining in all the rooms, as well as on the stairs and even in the garden. Clad in black tie, the adults were as mesmerized by the festivities as were Ivy's tiny costumed guests.

Ann is renowned for her cocktail buffets and the interesting assortment of hors d'oeuvres she serves. Although the guest list was extensive, all the food was cooked on site by Ann's chefs, and even for this army of people the selection and quality was nothing less than extraordinary.

The way one dresses or decorates a house should be reflective of one's personality, and entertaining should be, too. I find that the best party-givers are the people who see entertaining as a medium for their self-expression. No one does that better than Ann and Gordon Getty. Their style of entertaining is truly reflective of their unconventional spirits.

Rumaki

¼ cup soy sauce
2 16-ounce cans whole water chestnuts, drained
¼ cup brown sugar, loosely packed
1 teaspoon dry mustard powder
1 pound bacon, preferably center cut

Preheat the oven to 350°F.

In a large, shallow glass or ceramic dish, combine the soy sauce with the water chestnuts and allow to macerate for 15 minutes.

In another shallow dish, combine the brown sugar and the mustard, mixing well. Cut the bacon into 4-inch strips and dredge in the sugar mixture.

Drain the water chestnuts and wrap a strip of bacon around each. Place the wrapped water chestnuts on a foil-lined baking sheet. Bake for 15 to 20 minutes, or until the bacon is golden brown and bubbly. Remove from the oven and insert a toothpick into each water chestnut. Place on a serving platter and pass hot.

Rack of Lamb Gordon

Mustard and a crisp herbed crust make these chops irresistable. Be sure to french the bones or have your butcher do it so guests can treat the chops as finger food and get every delicious bitew.

SERVES 8 TO 10

¼ cup olive oil
¼ cup (½ stick) unsalted butter
4 racks of lamb (1½ pounds each, 7 to 8 chops
    per rack)
Salt to taste
1 cup fine bread crumbs
1 tablespoon chopped fresh thyme leaves
1 tablespoon chopped fresh oregano leaves
8 garlic cloves, minced
Freshly ground pepper to taste
1 cup Dijon mustard

Preheat the oven to 500°F.

In a 14 × 12 × 2-inch flameproof roasting pan, combine the oil and butter and place over high heat. Add the lamb racks and sear on all sides until brown, 3 to 4 minutes. Remove from the heat and season the lamb with salt.

Place the pan in the oven and roast the lamb on the center rack for 15 minutes for rare, 20 minutes for medium-rare. Remove from the oven and allow to rest for 10 minutes.

In a medium bowl, combine the bread crumbs, thyme, oregano, and garlic. Season with salt and pepper and mix thoroughly.

Generously smother the lamb racks with the mustard, making sure to coat between each chop. Sprinkle the lamb with the herbed bread crumbs and return to the oven for 5 minutes, until the crumbs have become a crust. Remove from the oven and carve the racks into individual chops. Serve 3 to 4 per person.

Jumbo Asparagus Persillé

SERVES 8

3½ pounds large asparagus, trimmed
1 tablespoon salt

BROWN BUTTER
1 cup (2 sticks) unsalted butter
¼ cup capers, drained
½ cup freshly grated Parmesan cheese

Using a vegetable peeler, peel the asparagus, starting about 1 inch below the tip. Using kitchen string, tie the spears into bunches of 6.

Fill a large saucepan half full with water and bring to a rapid boil. Add the salt and asparagus bunches and cook uncovered for 10 minutes. Use tongs to remove the bundles from the water. Cut and discard the strings.

While the asparagus cooks, make the brown butter. Melt the butter in a medium saucepan over low heat. Cook until it turns golden brown,

about 10 minutes. Remove from the heat immediately, transfer to a medium bowl, and stir in the capers.

Place 8 asparagus spears on each warm plate. Drizzle each portion with 2 tablespoons of brown butter and sprinkle with 1 tablespoon of Parmesan cheese.

Bebe Zecha

Jackie de Ravenal

Me &

CHRIS & GRACE MEIGHER

MICA ERTEGUN

More Friends

My Own Favorite: Pet de Nonne

SERVES 4 TO 6

The more formal name for this doughnut-like dessert is beignet soufflé, *but their ethereal lightness has earned them the nickname "nun's farts." My spectacular chef Sylvina makes them marvelously and serves them with two sauces. They're my very favorite dessert, and they're even good reheated for breakfast with jam.*

¼ teaspoon grated lemon zest
½ teaspoon salt
2 tablespoons unsalted butter
1 cup all-purpose flour
4 eggs
Vegetable oil for deep frying
Confectioner's sugar for dusting
Apricot Sauce (recipe follows)

In a saucepan, combine 1 cup water with the lemon zest, salt, and butter. Bring to a boil over medium heat. Remove from the heat and add the flour. Mix well, then place over low heat and cook, stirring constantly, until the mixture comes away from the sides of the pan and forms a ball. Add the eggs, one at a time, beating well after each addition.

In a deep fryer or heavy pot, heat the oil to 350°F. Using two spoons, form the dough into small balls the size of walnuts and drop 5 or 6 at a time into the hot oil. Deep fry until they puff and are golden brown on all sides, 3 to 4 minutes. Use a slotted spoon to transfer the balls to paper towels to drain. Sprinkle lightly with confectioner's sugar and serve hot with the sauce.

APRICOT SAUCE

20 dried apricots
½ cup sugar
2-inch piece of vanilla bean, split
1 tablespoon rum or brandy

In a saucepan, combine the apricots, sugar, and vanilla bean with 1 cup water. Bring to a boil over high heat. Reduce the heat and simmer for 20 minutes. Transfer to a blender and purée. Taste and add additional sugar if needed; if the sauce is too thick, add a bit more water. Just before serving, stir in the rum or brandy. Serve warm.

Bill Blass: Sour Cream Soufflé

SERVES 4

Everybody knows BB, and you can tell how much he loves food by looking at him, although he is shrinking as we speak. Bill is best suited to his country-squire mode and this is a taste. Served with smoked salmon, this makes a delicious first course.

1 tablespoon unsalted butter, softened
½ cup freshly grated Parmesan cheese
1¼ cups sour cream
½ cup sifted all-purpose flour
5 eggs, separated
1 teaspoon salt
¼ teaspoon cayenne pepper
2 tablespoons chopped fresh chives
2 egg whites

Preheat the oven to 350°F.

Butter a 2-quart soufflé dish. Dust the dish with 2 tablespoons of the Parmesan cheese, shake off the excess, and refrigerate the dish.

Pour the sour cream into a large mixing bowl and sift the flour into the sour cream. Thoroughly whip together with a wire whisk. Add the egg yolks one at a time, whisking briskly after each addition. Stir in the salt, cayenne pepper, chives, and the remaining Parmesan cheese.

Place all 7 egg whites in a large mixing bowl and beat, using a hand mixer, until stiff peaks form. Using a rubber spatula, gently fold the egg whites into the soufflé mixture. Pour the soufflé batter into the prepared soufflé dish and bake for 30 to 35 minutes, until the soufflé has risen 2 to 3 inches above the rim of the dish and is golden brown on top. Serve immediately.

Joy Henderiks: Waterzooi

SERVES 6 TO 8

Joy is my goddaughter and has my infectious disease of entertainitis. She has a knack for putting people together, filling every inch of her wonderful Paris apartment with friends who are attracted to her like bees to honey. She's fun!
This dish is a Belgian rendition of poule au pot, a rich, creamy stew that can also be made with fish.

1 chicken, cut into 8 serving pieces
1 celery stalk
2 leeks, white part only
2 carrots, peeled and cut into 2-inch pieces
1 large onion
2 sprigs of fresh flat leaf parsley
1 sprig of fresh thyme
1 bay leaf
1 sprig of fresh tarragon
4 rusks
¼ cup (½ stick) unsalted butter
¼ cup all-purpose flour
Juice of 1 lemon
Salt and freshly ground black pepper
¼ cup chopped fresh flat-leaf parsley

In a large saucepan, place the chicken pieces, celery, leeks, carrots, onion, parsley sprigs, thyme sprig, bay leaf, and tarragon sprig and add enough water to cover the ingredients. Bring to a simmer over medium-high heat, then cover tightly, reduce the heat, and cook gently for 2 hours.

Remove the chicken pieces to a bowl and set aside. Reserve the cooking liquid. Place the rusks in a small bowl and pour ½ cup of the cooking liquid over to soften. Using a slotted spoon, discard the herbs and transfer the vegetables to the bowl of a food processor with the softened rusks. Purée, then set aside.

In a medium saucepan, combine the butter and flour over medium heat, whisking to a smooth consistency. Add the remaining cooking liquid and the puréed vegetables and bring to a boil. Continue to cook, whisking continuously, until the mixture thickens and becomes smooth. Stir in the lemon juice and season with salt and pepper to taste.

Discard the skin and bones and cut the chicken into small pieces. Add the chicken to the sauce. Ladle the hot stew into individual bowls and garnish with the chopped parsley.

Bebe Zecha: Green Apple Tea

SERVES 4

My friend Bebe looks and sounds like a California coed. She's full of enthusiasm and so are her houses in Hong Kong and Bali. When Bebe makes this tea, she makes it by the barrel because no one can get enough. After a big meal it gives everyone sweet dreams and a cleansed palate.

1 Granny Smith apple
4 cups boiling water

Scrub the skin of the apple, core, and cut into 8 slices. Place in a teapot and pour in the boiling water. Steep for 10 minutes.

Serve after meals, with or without the apple slices.

Nancy Reagan: Currant Cookies

MAKES 36 COOKIES

Nancy is a foodie like me and we love to exchange recipes. She is known to have a weakness for cookies, and these are her absolute favorites.

½ cup (1 stick) butter
½ cup (1 stick) margarine
1 cup sugar
1 egg, beaten
2¼ cups all-purpose flour
2 teaspoons lemon extract
1 teaspoon grated lemon zest
1 cup dried currants

In a large mixing bowl, cream the butter and margarine together. Beat in the sugar until fluffy. Add the egg and stir in the flour, lemon extract, and lemon zest and mix until well blended. Stir in the currants and combine thoroughly. Chill the dough for 1 hour.

Preheat the oven to 350°F.

Grease 2 cookie sheets and drop the dough by teaspoonfuls 1 inch apart onto the sheets. Bake for 10 minutes, until golden brown. Remove to a wire rack to cool. These cookies can be stored in an airtight container for up to 2 weeks.

Nina Griscom: Bread and Butter Pudding

SERVES 10 TO 12

Tall, blond, beautiful, and shapely, Nina's looks belie her talent for cooking. Whether she whips up a fabulous lunch or dinner, her gatherings are always a "gabfest"!

¼ cup (½ stick) unsalted butter, softened
12 slices of good-quality white sandwich bread, crusts removed
½ teaspoon freshly grated nutmeg
1¼ cups raisins
4 large eggs, lightly beaten
1 cup milk
2 cups heavy cream
1 teaspoon vanilla extract
¾ cup confectioners' sugar
1½ tablespoons granulated sugar

Butter all the bread slices on one side with the softened butter. In an 8-inch square ceramic baking dish, arrange 4 slices buttered-side down. Sprinkle the bread with half of the nutmeg and half of the raisins and arrange another layer of bread, butter-side down, on top of the raisins. Sprinkle with the remaining nutmeg and raisins and top with the remaining 4 slices of bread buttered-side down.

In a medium bowl, whisk together the eggs, milk, cream, vanilla, and confectioners' sugar. Pour the mixture through a fine sieve over the bread. Sprinkle with the granulated sugar. Cover and let stand at room temperature for 1 hour, or refrigerate overnight.

Preheat the oven to 375°F.

Place the baking dish in a roasting pan and add enough hot water to reach halfway up the sides of the dish. Bake for 1 hour, until the pudding is crisp and golden on top and the custard is set. Serve warm with whipped cream or ice cream.

Grace & Chris Meigher: Key Lime Pie "Mirabile"

SERVES 8 TO 10

Dinner parties with the Meighers in Palm Beach are casual affairs—ties are forbidden, but bawdy stories encouraged! The ultimate course that never fails to solicit "oohs" and "aahs" from guests is their chef Brian Kenny's notoriously rich Key Lime Pie. Don't even think of tasting it without a sinful dollop of whipped cream.

CRUST

2¾ cups graham cracker crumbs
⅔ cups sugar
1 tablespoon ground cinnamon
¾ cup (1½ sticks) butter, melted

FILLING

8 egg yolks
2 (14-ounce) cans sweetened condensed milk
1¼ cups key lime juice
Finely grated zest of 1 key lime

Lightly sweetened whipped cream

Preheat the oven to 350°F.

In a large mixing bowl combine the graham cracker crumbs, sugar, and cinnamon. Add the butter and mix until well blended.

Press the crumb mixture onto the sides and bottom of a 10-inch springform pan. Bake for 6 to 8 minutes, or until golden brown. Remove from the oven and cool; do not turn off the oven.

While the crust bakes, beat the egg yolks with the condensed milk in a large bowl. Slowly add the lime juice, stirring constantly. Stir in the lime zest, then spoon the filling into the cooled shell. Bake for 8 to 10 minutes, or until the filling is set. Remove from the oven and cool to room temperature. Chill for 2 hours before serving with fresh whipped cream.

Kenneth J. Lane: Caspian Potato Salad

SERVES 6 TO 8

Kenny is famous not only for his entertaining but also for his jewelry, which he is inclined to give away to his friends—including lucky me! The last-minute addition of osetra caviar makes this salad decadent; fold in as much as you can afford—plus a bit more!

8 large new potatoes or Yukon Golds
4 cups dry white wine
3 tablespoons fresh lemon juice
½ cup olive oil
Freshly ground black pepper to taste
Osetra caviar

Place the potatoes in a large pot with water to cover and bring to a boil. Cook for 15 to 20 minutes, until the potatoes are tender but still firm. Drain and set aside to cool. Peel the potatoes and slice them into ¼-inch-thick slices. Place the slices in a large bowl, cover with the wine, and marinate for 30 minutes.

Meanwhile, prepare the vinaigrette. Place the lemon juice in a small bowl and slowly add the olive oil in a steady stream, whisking constantly until emulsified. Season with pepper.

Drain the potatoes and gently toss with the vinaigrette. Just before serving, gently fold in as much caviar as desired.

Mica Ertegun:
Turkish Artichokes

SERVES 6

Mica is the siren of the Turkish coast. Last time I was a guest of Mica and her husband, Ahmet, we rocked and rolled with Mick and Aretha! Mica entertains in different spots all over her house, setting lantern-lit tables on her roof garden, the back garden, drawing room, and living room. Even the breakfast trays are filled with delicious surprises, like Turkish yogurt with honey and figs.

2 tablespoons olive oil
3 medium onions, thinly sliced
2 small carrots, peeled and thinly sliced
2 celery stalks, diced
1 medium potato, peeled and diced
½ cup fresh peas
2 tablespoons all-purpose flour
Juice of 2 lemons
6 artichokes
½ cup chopped fresh dill
Salt to taste

Heat the olive oil in a large sauté pan over medium heat. Add the onions and cook for 5 minutes, stirring often, until translucent. Add the carrots, celery, and ½ cup of water and simmer for 20 minutes. Add the potato and peas and remove from the heat.

Fill a large bowl with cold water. Add the flour and half of the lemon juice. Remove the tough outer leaves of the artichokes until only the tender leaves remain. Using kitchen shears, trim off the sharp tips of the leaves and the stems of the artichokes and place the artichokes immediately in the lemon-water to prevent them from turning brown.

Drain the artichokes and add to the pot with the vegetables. Add 2 cups of water, the remaining lemon juice, and salt. Place a circle of parchment paper or wax paper directly on top of the artichokes and cook over medium heat for 40 minutes, until tender. Remove from the heat and allow the artichokes to cool in the pot. When cool enough to handle, use a spoon to scrape out the choke from the center of each.

Transfer the artichokes to a platter, fill the hearts with the mixed vegetables, and garnish with the fresh dill.

Jackie de Ravenel:
Baked Bahamian Crab

SERVES 4 TO 6

Jackie and her divine husband, Jean-Charles, exude charm, warmth, and joy. Their house in Nassau, where this decadent dish is often on the menu, is filled with treasures; it's fresh and cool and eyefilling. The food, too, is always breathtakingly good.

2 tablespoons olive oil
1 cup diced onions
1 cup diced carrots, blanched in boiling water for
   3 minutes (optional)
2 tomatoes, peeled and diced
½ cup diced red bell pepper
½ cup diced celery
½ pound mushrooms, diced
1 teaspoon fresh thyme leaves
Salt to taste
3 tablespoons unsalted butter
3 tablespoons all-purpose flour
1 cup fish stock
1 tablespoon tomato paste
Juice of one lemon
2 pounds fresh lump crabmeat, picked over
¼ cup toasted bread crumbs

Preheat the oven to 350°F. Butter a 2-quart ovenproof casserole.

Heat the oil in a large skillet over medium-high heat. Add the onions and sauté for 3 or 4 minutes, until translucent, then add the carrots, tomatoes, bell pepper, celery, mushrooms, and thyme. Cook, stirring, until the mushrooms and celery are softened and most of the liquid has evaporated. Season with salt to taste and set aside.

Melt the butter in a medium saucepan. Stir in the flour and cook over medium heat for a minute or two, stirring constantly. Add the fish stock all at once, stirring until smooth and thickened, then stir in the tomato paste. Season to taste with lemon juice.

Add the crab and sautéed vegetables and to the sauce and blend. Pour into the prepared dish, sprinkle with bread crumbs, and bake until golden, about 20 minutes.

Minnie Cushing Coleman: White Chocolate Pecan Pie

MAKES ONE 9-INCH PIE

Everybody in New Orleans knows and loves Minnie, and wants to be invited to her house because they know they'll have great food and a great time—a lot of giggles.

PASTRY

1¾ cups all-purpose flour
¼ cup finely ground pecans
¾ cup (1½ sticks) unsalted butter, chilled
2 to 4 tablespoons ice water

FILLING

½ cup sugar
¾ cup dark corn syrup
½ cup chopped white chocolate
2 cups pecan halves
2 eggs
½ teaspoon vanilla extract
2 tablespoons unsalted butter, melted
1 teaspoon cornstarch

Sift the flour into a large bowl and mix together with the ground pecans. Using your fingers and working quickly, incorporate the butter into the flour mixture until it resembles fine bread crumbs. Add the ice water a tablespoon at a time, tossing to combine, until the dough begins to hold together. Turn the mixture out onto a clean work surface and knead lightly just until smooth, about 1 minute. Flatten the dough into a disk and wrap in plastic. Chill for at least 30 minutes.

Combine the sugar and the corn syrup in a medium saucepan. Bring to a boil over a medium heat, stirring to dissolve the sugar, then reduce the heat to low and simmer for 2 minutes, stirring occasionally. Remove from the heat and cool completely, about 45 minutes.

Preheat the oven to 350°F. On a lightly floured surface, roll out the pie crust to a 13–inch circle about ⅛ inch thick. Grease a 9–inch pie pan and gently lay the dough in the pan. Crimp the edges with your fingers. Chill for 15 minutes.

Sprinkle the chopped chocolate evenly over the bottom of the crust and top with the pecan halves. In a large bowl, beat the eggs until foamy. Stir in the vanilla, melted butter, cooled syrup, and the cornstarch, and pour over the pecans.

Bake the pie for 40 minutes, or until the filling is set. Cool on a wire rack.

Pat Buckley: Betty's January Pudding

SERVES 6

Pat and her husband, Bill, spend every winter in Rougemont, next door to Gstaad in Switzerland. Bill writes up a storm and Pat entertains like mad. She's the hostess with the mostest, and has been known to get up in the middle of the night to make her famous oxtail soup. She and her wonderful chef Julien are a team to reckon with.

½ cup (1 stick) unsalted butter
½ cup dark brown sugar, packed
2 eggs, beaten
¼ cup raspberry jam
1 cup all-purpose flour
½ teaspoon baking soda
1 cup crème fraîche, lightly beaten
2 cups puréed raspberries

Butter a 2-quart glass bowl and set aside.

Cream the butter in a large mixing bowl with an electric beater. Beat in the sugar until light and fluffy. Add the eggs and combine, then beat in the jam until well blended. Add the flour and baking soda and beat until thoroughly incorporated.

Bring 2 to 3 inches of water to a boil in a pot large enough to hold the glass bowl. Pour the mixture into the prepared bowl, level the top, and place inside the pot of boiling water. Cover the pot and steam for 2 hours, checking occasionally to make sure the water has not boiled away; replenish the water as necessary.

Serve the pudding warm from the bowl, or cool it slightly and invert it onto a platter. Pass the crème fraîche and puréed raspberries separately.

Index